EAGLES ON
THEIR
BUTTONS

SHADES OF BLUE AND GRAY SERIES

*Edited by Herman Hattaway
and Jon Wakelyn*

The Shades of Blue and Gray Series will offer Civil War studies for the modern reader—Civil War buff and scholar alike. Military history today addresses the relationship between society and warfare. Thus biographies and thematic studies that deal with civilians, soldiers, and political leaders are increasingly important to a larger public. This series will include books that will appeal to Civil War Roundtable groups, individuals, libraries, and academics with a special interest in this era of American history.

EAGLES ON THEIR BUTTONS

A Black Infantry
Regiment in
the Civil War

Versalle F. Washington

University of Missouri Press
Columbia and London

Copyright © 1999 by
The Curators of the University of Missouri
University of Missouri Press, Columbia, Missouri 65201
Printed and bound in the United States of America
5 4 3 2 1   03 02 01 00 99

Library of Congress Cataloging-in-Publication Data

Washington, Versalle F., 1962
    Eagles on their buttons : a Black infantry regiment in the Civil
War / Versalle F. Washington.
        p.   cm. — (Shades of blue and gray series)
    Includes bibliographical references (p.   ) and index.
    ISBN 0-8262-1234-4 (alk. paper)
    1. United States. Army. Colored Infantry Regiment, 5th
(1863–1865) 2. United States—History—Civil War, 1861–1865—
Participation, Afro-American. 3. United States—History—Civil
War, 1861–1865—Regimental histories. 4. United States—History—
Civil War, 1861–1865—Social aspects. 5. Afro-American soldiers
Registers. I. Title. II. Series.
E492.94 5th.W37   1999
973.7'415—dc21   99-25130
                                                                CIP

⊗™ This paper meets the requirements of the
American National Standard for Permanence of Paper
for Printed Library Materials, Z39.48, 1984.

Text design: Stephanie Foley
Jacket design: Kristie Lee
Typesetter: Bookcomp, Inc.
Printer and binder: Thomson-Shore, Inc.
Typeface: Caslon 224

To my family

and to the men of the

5th Regiment, United States Colored Troops

CONTENTS

PREFACE

THE AMERICAN CIVIL WAR is a defining moment in the history of the United States. Northern victory restored the Union, but it also transformed the nature of the nation and brought significant changes to the country's African-American population. The events of the war brought freedom to 4 million blacks and forced the nation to reconsider the status of all its African-American inhabitants. These changes resulted from Constitutional amendment, executive orders, and the actions of Union soldiers.

The actions of Union soldiers, however, remain misrepresented in American military history. For a century after the war, many Americans believed that African Americans gained their freedom solely through the Emanciaption Proclamation and without any efforts of their own. They knew little or nothing of the struggle of African Americans, both in and out of uniform, to gain their rights. This is partly because few historians wrote on the subject of blacks' contributions during the war, although John Hope Franklin and Carter G. Woodson both wrote significant works on the general history of African Americans.[1]

The civil rights movement of the 1950s and 1960s sparked new interest in African-American history, encouraging historians such as Dudley Taylor Cornish, John Blassingame, and James McPherson to write about the lives of blacks in the Civil War. Of these, only Cornish focused on the military history of African-American units.[2]

Until recently, historians wrote little on the subject of black participation in the war. Even so, many of those who realize that blacks served in the Civil War still perceive African-American soldiers in the Union army to have been newly freed, largely illiterate, and primarily useful for fatigue and garrison duties. Black soldiers are not also thought of as Northerners who risked their lives and freedom to share in both the emancipation of their race and the victory of the Union. These thousands of men came from every Northern state as

ix

well as from Canada. Those who served in the Ohio regiments, while primarily Ohio residents, listed birthplaces in nearly every state in the Union and the Confederacy.

Despite the popular perception, African-American men from Ohio did serve, did fight, and did earn the praise of their superior officers, political supporters, and white comrades in the Union army. These black men were unique in some respects, but in most ways they were representative of the free blacks throughout the North during the 1860s.

Ohio African-American soldiers left comparatively few personal records. The National Archives contain some letters, but the primary location for their extant writings is in the newspapers of their time. Many abolitionist and Republican newspapers printed letters from these soldiers. The letters ranged from exhortations to descriptive works to condemnations of the treatment the soldiers received. With these letters to newspapers, the regiment's official documents, the letters from the archives, and the letters and diaries of some of the officers who led these men into battle, we can recreate the record of the 5th Infantry Regiment of United States Colored Troops (5th USCT) and perhaps see more clearly the larger picture of the American Civil War.

The Civil War took on a new aspect when the Union army accepted blacks into its ranks in early 1863. By the end of the war more than 180,000 black soldiers had fought for their country and for the freedom of their race. Two-thirds of these soldiers enlisted from the Confederate states. Nearly all of these had been slaves before the war. Although the South held nearly 4 million slaves, there were only 182,000 free African Americans of all ages and sexes throughout the South in 1860.[3] Other slaves who enlisted from Kentucky, Maryland, Delaware, and Missouri served with Union troops. The remaining 50,000 recruits came from the loyal states. These men were free, either having been born free in the North or having gained their freedom by manumission or escape from slavery.

The post–Civil War changes in the lives of the freedmen in the South are apparent, but African Americans in Ohio were free before the Civil War. These free African Americans did not have to fight for their liberty, nor did they have to fight for a nation that systematically denied them many of the rights of citizenship. In many ways, the benefits they could gain from volunteer military service were less than those to be gained by Southern freedmen or Northern whites. Yet when war erupted in 1861, African-American men in Ohio rushed to serve in Ohio's volunteer regiments, suggesting that they must have believed that their service could make a difference in their lives and in the lives of their people. Frederick Douglass provided a concise summary of this belief in his famous declaration, "Once let the black man get upon his person the brass letters 'US,' let him get an eagle on his button and a musket on his shoulder and bullets in his pockets and there is no power on earth which can deny that he has earned the right to citizenship in the United States."[4]

These African Americans found that even in time of war, only the most extreme need would cause white citizens to accept their black countrymen's offer of service. Military service, long required of Ohio's white citizens, was only one of the keys needed to open the door to equality for African Americans, but it was an essential one.

The belief that military service was indeed crucial to political and legal equality was a recurrent theme in the appeals for raising and recruiting the 5th USCT. John Mercer Langston, an African-American lawyer and the primary recruiter for the regiment, addressed this issue in his letters to Ohio Governor David Tod, in his speeches before the Union party and before black assemblies, and in his efforts to secure sympathetic officers to lead the regiment, once it was raised.

Langston had a clear understanding of the legal problems confronting African Americans in Ohio. He had defended blacks in court, sometimes overcoming the inherently unbalanced system. He had seen his brother go to prison for violating the Fugitive Slave Law. He had been a vociferous advocate of African-American suffrage and saw the acceptance of blacks on the battlefield as another step on that road.

Much of what made the Northern USCT and state-sponsored black regiments different from the black regiments raised in the South was the activism of the abolitionist community. The 5th USCT had strong ties to the Oberlin antislavery community. Langston's style of rhetoric reflected abolitionist concerns and concerns for gaining political equality through service. These were precepts of the Oberlin community.

The Oberlin influence manifested itself most clearly in Giles Shurtleff, an Oberlin divinity student and former captain of Company C, 7th Ohio Volunteer Infantry (OVI). This company contributed two other officers to the regiment, and five other Oberlinites served as officers in the 5th USCT. Additionally, the two primary recruiters for the regiment were from Oberlin. Few of the 5th USCT's enlisted men were from Oberlin because many of Oberlin's eligible blacks, like those from the rest of the state, had previously left Ohio to serve in the 54th and 55th Massachusetts regiments.

In 1863, Ohio's African-American men finally received the chance to serve as soldiers in the Union army, but they did so under adverse conditions. They were often treated with scorn by white soldiers, segregated into the units of the United States Colored Troops, paid less (for much of the war) than other soldiers, and denied hope of advancement into the officer ranks. Despite these facts and the scant hope for equality, Ohio's African-American soldiers fought and died for more than two years, serving with honor and distinction.

Historians have told the stories of some colored regiments. The 54th Massachusetts Volunteer Infantry Regiment is one of the most famous Civil War units. We know about the exploits of the 1st South Carolina Volunteer Infantry Regiment and Colonel Thomas Wentworth Higginson. We understand the educational advantages that freedmen gained while serving in the USCT regiments.[5]

However, we know little of the Northern blacks who served in the USCT. Yet the gallant Ohioans who served as the 5th USCT Regiment had a distinguished record. The 5th Infantry Regiment of United States Colored Troops was one of the 163 African-American regiments that the Union government raised to help fight the Civil War. The 5th USCT was unique in several aspects. It was one of the thirty-three regiments raised by the free states of the Union and the ninth such regiment to begin mustering in troops. Its combat record is impressive. For many reasons, including some commanders' reluctance to commit colored troops to battle and the prevalent use of USCT soldiers for fatigue duties, few of the colored regiments fought in major battles. The 5th USCT fought in three battles and engaged Confederates in four other skirmishes.[6] The 5th USCT is also distinguished by having had four of the army's sixteen African-American recipients of Civil War Medals of Honor in its ranks.

An examination of the 5th USCT will show what caused the men to join the regiment, what sort of men they were, and how they fought and lived as African-American soldiers in the Civil War. It will bring to light the rhetoric, recruiting, and motivations of the soldiers and officers and will demonstrate the struggles of the regiment against rebel forces in North Carolina and Virginia. It will also illustrate that the 5th USCT, which had four Medal of Honor recipients and fought with distinction at Petersburg and New Market Heights, was one of the finest regiments of the war.

In the decades following the Civil War, no group of Union soldiers received less attention than the men of the USCT. In the century between the end of the Civil War and the publication of Dudley Taylor Cornish's *The Sable Arm,* only three book-length studies on the USCT were published—William Wells Brown, *The Negro in the American Rebellion, 1861–1865* (1867); Joseph T. Wilson, *The Black Phalanx* (1888); and George Washington Williams, *A History of Negro Troops in the War of the Rebellion* (1888)—and these were printed before the completion of the *Official Record,* which contained the government's documents regarding the war.[7] USCT veterans, eager to lionize their comrades-in-arms, wrote two of the three works, so it is unsurprising that they lacked objectivity. The works' most critical flaw, however, was that these authors lacked access to government documents.

Since Taylor's work, a number of historians have tackled the history of the USCT. The last seven years have seen the publication of at least five new works: Hondon Hargrove, *Black Union Soldiers in the Civil War* (1988); William Gladstone, *United States Colored Troops, 1863–1867* (1991); Joseph Glatthaar, *Forged in Battle* (1991); Howard Westwood, *Black Troops, White Commanders, and Freedmen during the Civil War* (1992); and Gladstone, *Men of Color* (1993).

Hargrove, Gladstone, and Glatthaar look at the entire USCT, while Westwood offers selected vignettes. *Black Union Soldiers in the Civil War* is too short to provide adequate coverage of the USCT, but it does highlight critical events. *United States Colored Troops, 1863–1867* and *Men of Color* are photographic histories of the USCT. Although both are quite informative, they are primarily encyclopedic, rather than analytic, works. *Forged in Battle,* easily the best of the three, is carefully researched and well written. However, Glatthaar concentrates more on the experiences of the freedman enlistee than on those USCT soldiers entering as free men from the North.

The motivations of the free black volunteer for service, his conduct during the war, and the associations he formed with the white officers who led him into battle were different from those of the "contraband," or freedman enlistee. For many contrabands, the army was an escape from slavery, a ready source of employment, and a chance to take up arms against their former masters. The free black volunteers did not share these motivations. They viewed the army as an opportunity to prove their worth as men and as an argument for gaining equal rights under the law. The men of the 5th USCT were free. Their regiment consisted primarily of men recruited in Ohio, most of whom gave Ohio locations as their homes. This is a study of these men. It will examine their condition before the war to determine the reasons they had for joining the Union army, the officers who tied their fortunes to those of the black soldiers, the conduct of the soldiers in the war, and the results of their wartime service.

ACKNOWLEDGMENTS

THIS WORK WOULD NOT have been possible without the help of many people. Professor Allan Millett, my adviser, mentor, and friend, suggested this topic and has been a patient source of inspiration and guidance throughout. Professor Williamson Murray provided encouragement to begin studying military history. Professor Mark Grimsley kept me from making egregious stumbles as I researched and wrote, for which I am grateful. Any errors that still remain are, of course, my own. As I researched, I received help in the form of suggestions and criticism from Professor Richard Smith. Michel Perdreau and Timothy Oren generously allowed me to use materials in their possession and shared their knowledge of the regiment and its history. Professor Roland Baumann and his staff at the Oberlin College Archives rose far above the call of duty to help me. I also received timely advice from the staffs at the National Archives, Army Military History Institute, Delaware County Historical Society, Ohio Historical Society, and Wilberforce University.

Special thanks are in order for the efforts of James Johnson and Herman Hattaway, who made the leap of faith necessary to bring this book to pass. I also must thank Beverly Jarrett, Jane Lago, Julie Schorfheide, and the rest of the editorial staff at the University of Missouri Press for turning this work around so quickly.

My family has provided a rich source of support and love. I thank Dr. Eugene Lundy and the congregation of the Church of Christ of the Apostolic Faith for their prayers. I thank my wife, Kathleen, for her patience, love, care, and understanding throughout this process. As ever, I give thanks to God for allowing me to have this opportunity.

EAGLES ON
THEIR
BUTTONS

1

Raising the Regiment

THE 5TH USCT BEGAN forming companies at Camp Delaware in central Ohio in June 1863. This formation was the culmination of years of effort by blacks and whites, working together to raise black regiments to help put down the rebellion in the Confederate states. The men who wanted to see African Americans in uniform had reasons as varied as the men who volunteered for service. Some wanted to put down the rebellion at all costs and believed that the black soldier was just another weapon to that end. Some believed that since soldiering was a duty of citizens, having black soldiers would lead to having black citizens. Some African Americans believed that war was a proper pursuit for men and that service would prove their manhood. That these viewpoints coalesced and led to the formation of the 5th USCT Regiment is a testimony to the intensity with which they were held.

Although the men of the 5th USCT mustered into service during the latter half of 1863, Ohio's African-American men had been trying to volunteer for service from the beginning of the war. These men, who daily dealt with the open contempt of many of their countrymen, were ready to help defend a government that had recently declared that a black man had no rights a white man was bound to acknowledge and that had adopted a fugitive slave law, which effectively opened them and their families to kidnapping and transportation into slavery.[1]

The government they were willing to defend, however, showed no interest in their assistance. Both the federal and Ohio governments turned down offers from African Americans and their supporters. These took the form of ready organized units, offers to raise units, suggestions for the use of African-American men in the war effort,

1

and individual requests, from prominent and private black men, to serve.

Like so many Ohioans, these men were willing to enlist in the early rush of the war frenzy. Failing in this, they still pressed for the Union to allow them to fight when it became clear that the war would be neither quick nor bloodless. These men clamored for two years for their right to fight before conditions in the war led the Lincoln administration to allow the recruitment of African-American soldiers. After many of Ohio's black men left the state to serve in the Massachusetts regiments, those who remained argued for the right to serve in an Ohio black regiment. Their chance finally would come, but one needs to examine their struggle to gain the right to serve to understand the fervor and determination they exhibited in uniform.

One of the earliest attempts by Ohio's African-American men to join in the war demonstrates their eagerness to contribute and the persistence of blacks to serve as Union soldiers. At the war's outbreak, 115 black men were studying at Wilberforce University in southwestern Ohio. The Methodist Episcopal Conference and the African Methodist Episcopal Conference had jointly established Wilberforce in 1856 to educate and train African-American students. These students formed a company and volunteered their services to Ohio Governor William Dennison. He rejected their offer. Many of these men later served with the 54th Massachusetts.[2]

Ohio's governor did not want the services of Ohio's African-American citizens, but this rejection did not prevent them from continuing their offers. At a meeting of blacks in Cleveland in 1861, those in attendance announced their continued support for the war effort and swore loyalty to the government, despite acknowledging that under it they "enjoy[ed] the blessings of personal, though not political, freedoms." They resolved to protect this government with their property, their prayers, and their lives.[3]

Ohioans elected David Tod to the governor's mansion, and black leaders renewed their attempts to raise a black regiment in the state. Early in 1862 John Mercer Langston, a prominent African American and Oberlin College graduate, asked Governor Tod for permission to raise African-American regiments. Governor Tod refused his request, saying, "This is a *white man's* government; that white men are able to defend and protect it, and that to enlist a negro soldier would be to drive every white man out of the service." Langston recalled that he replied, "Governor, when you need us, send for us."[4]

Governor Tod had good reasons for rejecting Langston's request. The United States government was not yet accepting African-American units into federal service, and Irishmen in Cincinnati threatened mob violence if Ohio enlisted blacks.[5] The governor also followed a precedent set in Ohio in 1803 that barred African Americans from militia service.

This 1803 act was one of many Ohio laws aimed at its African-American inhabitants. Blacks in Ohio could expect a wide range of treatment from the state's white residents. Since much of the state's commerce was with the South, and because many Ohioans in the southern part of the state had come from the South, racist prejudices and practices were firmly entrenched in that area. The northern portion of the state was home to people who for the most part had emigrated from New England, New York, and Pennsylvania. Many of these settlers shared the Congregationalist and Quaker roots of their eastern relatives. These religions viewed slavery as a blight on the nation, and both churches actively helped escaping slaves. While the area was not without its racist citizens, northern Ohio's strong abolitionist community kept its residents from excessively concerning themselves with creating laws to restrict the rights of blacks.

Northern Ohio was progressive in its educational policies for African Americans. This portion of the state housed Oberlin College, which admitted African Americans to its student body and allowed them to gain a higher education. Cleveland, which had a black population of just 772 in 1860, had integrated schools and some African-American teachers.

Ohio's first state legislature, however, took steps to ensure that white Ohioans enjoyed greater status than African Americans. In 1802 the legislature passed, by a narrow margin, a law granting suffrage only to white males.[6] Article 8 of the constitution, which passed by a single vote, prohibited slavery in the state.[7] While Ohio blacks would be free, their status was similar to that of Native Americans. The state government offered them protections under the law, but they could take no part in making that law.

By 1804, the influx of blacks from the South raised concerns in southern Ohio that the region would be overrun with black settlers.

In response to these concerns, the legislature enacted the first of a series of laws that circumscribed the freedoms and rights of blacks in Ohio. After 1804, African Americans had to furnish proof of their free status and to register their families with the clerk of the county in which they wished to reside. This law also made it a crime to hire blacks who could not furnish proof of free status. After 1807, blacks wishing to move to Ohio could only do so upon paying a $500 bond and having two bondsmen sign for their support and good behavior. In 1807, the legislature reenacted a provision of the law that prohibited African Americans from testifying against whites in a court of law.

Officials did not evenly enforce these Black Laws. In Cincinnati, for example, the bond requirement was not enforced until 1829, when city officials, alarmed by the rapid growth in the African-American population, gave blacks thirty days to present their bonds and fees. When the city failed to collect the required bonds, a mob attacked the black citizens, who barricaded themselves in their homes and repulsed the mob for three days. After the mob dispersed, more than 2,200 African Americans left Cincinnati for Canada.[8]

The most pernicious of the enforced Black Laws excluded blacks from the public schools. Ohio established a system of public schools in 1821 but did not have a uniform tax law to fund the schools until 1825. Initially, the law did not exclude African Americans from the schools, but prevalent prejudice kept them out of schools in most areas of Ohio. Although few blacks attended school, the state still levied property taxes for black-owned properties. The Ohio legislature remedied this unfair practice in 1829, not by compelling schools to admit African-American students, but by prohibiting blacks from attending public schools and, in concert with this act, by calling for local governments to use all property taxes collected from African Americans solely for the instruction of black pupils. For the next two decades, those blacks who received an education in Ohio did so through the assistance of philanthropic organizations and abolitionist groups or through the efforts of the black communities in the larger cities.[9]

The Ohio legislature repealed the Black Laws in 1849, but Ohioans saw few changes after the legislation's modification. Blacks still attended separate schools, could not vote or serve on juries, and were excluded from the militia.

The last of the disadvantages facing Ohio's African-American citizens in the years before the Civil War was the persistent stream of petitions calling for the removal of blacks from the state. In 1850, 135 citizens of Butler County signed such a document. This petition did, however, request that the blacks be compensated for the loss of their property. During the 1850 debates on revisions to the state constitution, petitions favoring the prohibition of African-American immigration and forced colonization of Ohio's blacks came before the legislature as frequently as three times a day. Nearly all the petitions came from the southern half of the state.[10]

Ohio law and Ohio's social practices gave its African-American citizens little reason to believe that the government belonged to them, as it did to the white man. The government refused to acknowledge the rights of black citizens. It gave them no voice in changing the law, no equal protection in the enforcement of the law, and little hope that this situation would be changed. Yet when the Civil War brought the call to arms, Ohio's African-American men answered the call—promptly and persistently.

The motivation of these African-American men merits closer attention. Joseph Glatthaar stated that "like Northern whites, [Northern blacks] were citizen soldiers who stepped forward in time of national crisis."[11] Northern blacks, however, dealt with a different set of rules, rules that excluded them from most obligations and privileges of citizens. The desire to gain the benefits and duties of citizenship was one of the primary motivations held out to prospective recruits.

Newspapers of the period provide insight into the rhetoric that both sides used in the fight to enlist African-American soldiers. While white regiments fought the Confederates during the first two years of the war, abolitionists, blacks, and others who wanted to see black soldiers in the Union army fought a fierce battle of words in the various presses. Abolitionist newspapers like the *Liberator, Pine and Palm, National Anti-Slavery Standard,* and the *Christian Recorder* joined with Republican newspapers such as the *Ohio State Journal* and the (Cincinnati) *Gazette* to battle with the Ohio's Democrat newspapers, including *Crisis* and the (Cincinnati) *Enquirer* for the hearts and minds of Ohioans.

The abolitionist newspapers, while banned in several Southern states, had a national scope. They maintained a local flavor by

printing letters, editorials, and news items sent in by their read-
ers. Ohioans took advantage of the newspapers' policies to draw
attention to their efforts to join in the struggle, to encourage African
Americans to join when the opportunity arose, and, in some cases, to
deter black participation. An early example of the latter appeared in
Pine and Palm on May 25, 1861. The unnamed correspondent, who
wrote from Chillicothe, argued that the hope of African-American
enfranchisement resulting from black participation in the war was
absurd, warning that "if the colored people, under all the social and
legal disabilities by which they are environed, are ever ready to
defend the government that despoils them of their rights, it may
be concluded that it is quite safe to oppress them." The writer
further noted that the efforts of African Americans in the Revo-
lutionary War and in the War of 1812 had not gained them their
rights as citizens.[12] Northern blacks were no more united in their
response to the war than were Northern whites. Only two weeks
before this letter appeared in *Pine and Palm*, the *Liberator* printed
an article concerning a meeting of Cleveland's African-American
men, who resolved that "to-day, as in the times of '76 and the
days of 1812, we are ready to go forth and do battle in the common cause of the country."[13] Ohio's blacks continued to meet and
discuss the war, their role in it, and their possibilities upon its
conclusion.

Still, Ohio's blacks chafed to do something concrete to aid the
Union cause. W. E. Ambush, an African American from Cleveland,
wrote to Governor Tod, offering the services of black regiments, not
to fight, but simply to relieve the white regiments standing guard at
Johnson Island and at Camp Chase, two prisoner-of-war camps. Ambush argued that using the black regiments in this way would enable
loyal African-American men to serve their government, would free
up the white regiments for more active service, and would avoid
the complaints of those white soldiers who did not wish to serve
alongside colored companies. Governor Tod declined even this offer,
claiming that he had no authority to use colored troops to guard
rebel prisoners.[14]

Although Governor Tod was reluctant to use African-American
soldiers to defend the "white man's government," other leaders
had fewer difficulties with the idea. Under the auspices of staunch
antislavery advocates, black regiments began mustering in Kansas,
Louisiana, and South Carolina.

Kansas, a state that had seen violent clashes over slavery, was among the first to muster black soldiers. Kansas Senator James H. Lane gave up his Senate seat to accept a volunteer commission as a brigadier general. He recruited and organized a regiment of escaped slaves in Leavenworth, Kansas. On January 13, 1863, this regiment, the 1st Kansas Colored Volunteers (later the 79th USCT), became the first Northern black regiment accepted into Federal service. Cornish noted that Lane had integrated African Americans into his white cavalry regiment as early as October 1861.[15]

Free blacks in Louisiana gained acceptance into Federal ranks even before the 1st Kansas Colored Volunteers. Although the 1st Kansas was the first African-American regiment to fight, the 1st, 2nd, and 3rd Louisiana Native Guards preceded them into Federal uniforms. General Ben Butler mustered the 1st Louisiana Native Guards into Federal service on September 27, 1862, five days after Lincoln announced his Emancipation Proclamation. The Louisiana Native Guards added to the strong tradition of New Orleans's free colored population. Their units had suffered under the Confederate government, which had disbanded and disarmed them. These men claimed the right to serve based on nearly unbroken service from 1727. Louisiana was the only state that had colored militia in 1803, and two of these companies fought under Andrew Jackson in the War of 1812.[16]

Butler took advantage of the South's largest prewar population of free blacks to raise his three regiments. By July 1862, other Union army commanders took advantage of the Contraband Laws to enlist escaped slaves into the army, mostly as laborers, but also as soldiers. The Contraband Laws were the popular names of the First and Second Confiscation Acts, which gave the Federal government increased powers to take property, including slaves, of people living in the rebel states.[17] Notable among the commanders who seized the opportunity was General David Hunter, who took advantage of the First Contraband Law to declare that all blacks in the Department of the South (South Carolina, Georgia, and Florida) were free. Lincoln quickly revoked Hunter's action, declaring, "Neither General Hunter nor any other commander or person has been authorized by the Government of the United States to make proclamations declaring the slaves of any State free."[18]

Hunter failed because of his impatience and unwillingness to keep the government aware of his actions. President Lincoln did not like to be surprised by the actions of his subordinates. By August 6, Lincoln ended Hunter's hopes of maintaining a South Carolina regiment by refusing to authorize officers or pay for the African Americans.[19] A disgusted General Hunter disbanded the regiment on August 10. Two weeks later, Secretary of War Edwin M. Stanton authorized General Rufus Saxton, an abolitionist, to raise African-American soldiers. However, because General Hunter had not been able to keep his promises of pay, arms, uniforms, and recognition as soldiers to the first group of enlistees, General Saxton had a difficult time convincing blacks of the government's sincerity. Colonel Higginson took command in November, but the 1st South Carolina Volunteers did not gain acceptance into the army until January 1863. Despite this, the unit was the first raised, with or without official sanction, by agents of the United States government.

Ohio's earliest experiments with using blacks for military labor started inauspiciously. In September 1862, General Lew Wallace, military commander of Cincinnati, declared martial law in preparation for an attack by Confederate forces under the command of General John Hunt Morgan. Although the city's blacks had been excluded from the martial law declaration, the city police, armed with bayonets, began rounding up African-American men and then marched them to the fortifications taking shape on the hills outside of Covington, Kentucky, across the river from the city. Although the defenders gave up significant advantages by not incorporating the Ohio River in their defense, their desire to keep rebel forces completely outside the state dictated the position of the city's defenses. The black men's families had no idea why the men had been taken and sought to find them. General Wallace learned of the blacks' dilemma and took steps to stop the press gangs.

General Wallace ordered Judge William M. Dickson to organize the city's African-American men as laborers to construct fortifications. Judge Dickson reclaimed the African Americans, many of whom had been taken to nearby Union camps to become servants, and allowed them to return home while he arranged for their work. The blacks worked digging trenches and rifle pits for two weeks, often laboring in front of the city's defenders. These men, who became known as the Black Brigade of Cincinnati, received unit colors and were organized into companies under African-American officers. They were clearly a military labor rather than a combat organization but were nonetheless the first such organization in the Northern states.[20]

The Emancipation Proclamation renewed the hope of African-American men who wanted to fight for the Union, since the document provided for the enlistment of African-American men. Again Ohio blacks flocked to join Union forces. Again they were disappointed. Massachusetts, however, soon began to raise black regiments. Black Ohioans went in large numbers to Massachusetts to join these regiments.

Early in 1863, Massachusetts Governor John Andrew obtained permission from Secretary Stanton to raise a brigade of African-American soldiers. Andrew, an ardent abolitionist, wanted to bring African Americans into the Union army, even though Massachusetts did not have a sufficiently large black population to man a regiment. Since his state's African-American population was so small, Andrew recruited African-American soldiers throughout the North, especially in Ohio. Governor Tod supported these actions and even had Ohio's recruiters assist in raising troops for the 54th and 55th Massachusetts Volunteer Infantry Regiments.[21]

However, in his letter to Langston of May 16, 1863, Governor Tod made it clear that he still had no intention of raising an Ohio regiment of African-American soldiers.[22] He reiterated this point to prospective commanders of such a unit in a series of letters throughout May and the first two weeks of June. On May 27, however, Tod asked Stanton for permission to raise an African-American Ohio volunteer regiment.[23]

Tod's reversal involved several factors. He had originally been a war Democrat but had won the Union Party's nomination for governor. As a Union Party governor, he supported the war effort, but not necessarily the antislavery issue so closely bound to the war. Union casualties and the length of the war added to the pressure for Northern states, including Ohio, to provide more soldiers. Unless Ohio supplied the Union with volunteer regiments, the Federal government would draft Ohioans into the service. Enlisting blacks, therefore, became a possible way for Ohio to avoid the draft. The successful recruiting for the Massachusetts regiments made it clear that Ohio had resources that it had not yet employed. The *Ohio State Journal* reported in May 1863 that nearly nine hundred

African-American volunteers had passed through Cleveland that month, destined for the Massachusetts regiments.[24]

Langston, who played a major role in recruiting for the two Massachusetts regiments as well as for the 5th USCT, toured Ohio to speak to groups of African-American citizens. His speech in Cincinnati in May 1863 addressed "the position of the colored men of the country and . . . their duty of sustaining with life, if needed, the Government which had done so much for them."[25] Langston believed that service in the war would obligate the government to consider the rights of its black citizens. Langston apparently had good reason to believe this. In a letter printed in the *Liberator,* Governor Andrew cited Secretary Stanton as saying that

> he would never consent that free colored men should be accepted into the service to serve as soldiers in the South, until he should be assured that the Government of the United States was prepared to guarantee and defend, to the last dollar and the last man, to these men all the rights, privileges, and immunities that are given, by the laws of civilized warfare, to other soldiers. Their present acceptance and muster-in as soldiers, pledges the honor of the nation in the same degree and to the same rights with all other troops. They will be soldiers of the Union—nothing less and nothing different. I believe they will earn for themselves an honorable fame, vindicating their race and redeeming their future from the aspersions of the past.[26]

Andrew, as an abolitionist, viewed the plight of African Americans with more compassion than most of his contemporaries. This sympathy for blacks is evident in his persistent efforts to raise and support African-American regiments. He would have been expected to make extraordinary efforts on behalf of his state's black regiments. However, for African-American men who desired to enlist in Ohio, only a promise from the national government would be of any consequence. Consequently, Secretary Stanton's remarks must have been especially welcome because he had not previously shown any sympathy for African Americans.

Cleveland blacks, willing to do whatever was necessary to join in the struggle, resolved to form companies of men to conduct military drill, as "it is evident that it will be necessary whether they go from the State or from Massachusetts."[27] Governor Tod recognized that he was allowing a valuable asset to leave his state. He asked Secretary

Stanton for permission to raise African-American regiments, but Stanton insisted that Ohio should not begin to recruit soldiers until the Massachusetts regiments were full.

Many of Ohio's African Americans did not share Langston's faith in Ohio's government. When Governor Tod announced that Ohio would recruit its own regiment of colored infantry, some still wanted to enlist in the Massachusetts regiments, which offered a bounty and promised higher pay. Tod hoped to counter this sentiment by announcing that "whatever had been the case in months gone by, henceforth the colored man will be treated in every respect as an equal of the white."[28] Clearly, Tod's statement meant only that African-American and white soldiers would receive the same items from the government, as no government had the power to compel social equality. The *Cleveland Leader* article clarified Tod's intent in a later paragraph that specifically equated the 127th Ohio Volunteer Infantry's rations, bounties, pay, and equipment with that of the state's white regiments.[29]

While equal treatment as soldiers certainly would have improved the lot of those who chose to enlist, it could not have been sufficient incentive for most of Ohio's African-American population. Nor was the money that the soldiers earned the primary incentive. As a correspondent to the *Christian Recorder* noted, the ten dollars a month that soldiers earned was not as much as an able-bodied black could have earned working as a farm laborer. The writer also wryly pointed out that laborers faced few cannonballs and could be home with their families while earning their money.[30] However, it was not money that these soldiers sought. Their motivations were hopes of preserving the Union, defeating slavery, gaining a chance for political equality, and proving their worthiness for the gains they would be making for their race.

Popular opinion in Ohio concerning the enlistment of African-American soldiers was mixed, with little apparent pattern to viewpoints. The Democratic press, however, united in opposition to the idea. The (Cincinnati) *Enquirer* warned,

> The employment of negro soldiers is . . . *a disgrace to the Government that employs them—a reproach to our cause—calculated to bring upon us the shame of the whole world,* and to cause the South to fight as one man against us. The negro is a barbarian. His method of making war is by the destruction

and massacre of women and children, as well as men, by the
perpetration of atrocities that makes humanity shudder.[31]

The (Columbus) *Crisis,* noting that Union General Hunter was
conscripting freedmen in South Carolina, wrote, "When the abolitionists are compelled to resort to conscription to get the negroes
into the army to fight for their liberty they might as well give the
chase up."[32]

These Democrat newspapers used two of the popular arguments
against enlisting African Americans into the Union army. Many
Ohioans believed, as Governor Tod had so clearly stated, that military pursuits were properly the domain of white citizens. Other
white Ohioans believed that the blacks either would not or could not
fight, particularly according to any known conventions of warfare.
President Lincoln made the first of these arguments moot with the
Emancipation Proclamation's provision for enlisting blacks into the
service. It remained for the African-American soldiers to dismiss
the second argument.

No one needed to conscript Ohio's African Americans to serve
as soldiers. Governor Tod received permission to raise an African-
American regiment from Secretary Stanton on June 16; on June 22,
the first members of the 127th Ohio Volunteer Infantry Regiment
(Colored) mustered into the Union ranks. Despite the enthusiasm
of the African-American soldiers, many Ohioans still were unsure
of their value. John Brough, a Union Party gubernatorial candidate,
took the pragmatic view, asking Ohio's white citizens, "Why should
[African-American soldiers'] blood be saved in war more than that of
the whites? If they are willing to go when you ain't willing to go, why
should you stand and cavil?"[33] Regardless of the concerns of their
white neighbors, the soldiers streamed into Camp Delaware. Within
the first five weeks of the recruiting period, nearly four hundred soldiers had mustered into service.[34] The recruiting, although uneven,
went well enough for the regiment to be ready for service by the end
of September. This was a remarkable achievement, considering the
number of Ohio's eligible African-American men that had already
enlisted in the Massachusetts regiments.

As in every other stage in raising black soldiers in Ohio, Langston
played a key role. Governor Tod, recognizing Langston's valuable
efforts in encouraging African Americans from the Midwest to enlist

in the two Massachusetts black regiments, appointed Langston as chief recruiter for the Ohio African-American regiment. Tod also appointed Langston's partner, O. S. B. Wall, as general recruiting agent.

Recruiting in Ohio should have been a thankless job. Since recruiters received two dollars for every recruit, recruiting could be lucrative, especially if the state made enlistment attractive by providing bounties. However, unlike Massachusetts, Ohio offered no bounties for the men who were to enlist in the state's first colored regiment. Langston and former governor William Dennison, a Republican, tried to raise money for bounties through private subscriptions, but this effort was largely a failure. While recruiters for white soldiers could offer Federal bounties of forty dollars, the money raised by Dennison's private fund could offer less than three dollars to the black recruit. By mid-September, there was not enough of the fund left to continue paying for the services of recruiters. Soldiers such as Milton Holland, orderly (or first) sergeant of C Company, found themselves pressed into recruiting duty to save the state two dollars per recruit.[35]

Unlike most volunteer regiments, the 5th USCT recruited soldiers throughout the state. Langston and Wall personally canvassed the state to find recruits and organized other recruiting agents to assist them in their effort. These agents recruited the soldiers, often by holding large gatherings at which prominent African-American citizens or Ohio government officials would give rousing speeches.

Wall spoke in Athens in July 1863. Like Langston, Wall was from Oberlin, where he owned a shoemaking business. He portrayed the Civil War as an opportunity for the black man to show his worthiness for equality and liberty. He believed that his fellow blacks should "join in the work of elevation of the race from degradation to equality," thereby "conferring the boon of freedom on their fellow men of the South, and of elevation to the entire race." Wall strove to impress upon his listeners the historic impact of their decisions. He concluded by saying, "If the colored citizens of Ohio are such men as they aspire to be, now is the time to show it."[36]

Another meeting, held in Xenia on August 4 and 5, 1863, featured Langston. His speech, entitled "The Hour and the Duty of Colored Men to the Government," inspired the African Americans to adopt a resolution promising to fill the remaining two companies of the

regiment. This resolution also stated that the colored citizens of
Ohio would stand by the government and pledge their "lives, [their]
property, and [their] sacred honor" to defeat the Confederacy and
assist the government in its effort "to recognize the citizenship of
the native-born colored American."[37] This resolution shows that in
the minds of these African-American Ohioans military service and
full citizenship remained inextricably entwined.

Pride and sense of manhood were strong motivators for many of
Ohio's African-American men. Richard Cain noted, "We knew that
there would come a period in the history of this nation when our
strong black arms would be needed."[38] Orderly Sergeant Holland
exhorted the men who had not yet enlisted to

> spring forth to the call, and show the world that you are men.
> You have thus far shown, and still continue to show yourselves
> worthy of freedom, and you will win the respect of the whole
> nation. There is a brighter day coming for the colored man, and
> he must sacrifice home comforts, and his blood, if necessary,
> to speed the coming of that glorious day.[39]

The men who volunteered for the African-American regiment
were typical of Ohio's black men. For them, antebellum economic
opportunities were few. Most black Ohioans lived in the country
or in small towns; African-American population in Ohio's cities
was small. Cincinnati had 3,731 black inhabitants, but this figure
was nearly 3,000 higher than any other city population in the
state.[40] Because of these low concentrations, African Americans
were seldom able to support their own business enterprises.

Since they had few alternatives, blacks generally took jobs as do-
mestics and menials in cities and as farmers or laborers in the country. The soldiers' occupations before the war followed this pattern.
Over half of the African-American soldiers listed their occupation as
farmer (53 percent). The next most common occupation among the
5th USCT's recruits was laborer (22 percent). Other prominent jobs
were boatman (2 percent), waiter (2 percent), and cook (1 percent).
Soldiers with skilled trades included barbers (4 percent), black-
smiths (3 percent), carpenters (1 percent), coopers (1 percent),
and masons (1 percent). In all, the soldiers listed more than fifty
distinct occupations, including engineer, servant, painter, teacher,
minister, and doctor. Only six of the men claimed no occupation.

Some privileged blacks lived in Ohio. Church and philanthropic individuals sponsored African Americans, providing them with land, manumission, or, in some cases, the opportunity to attend private schools. One such beneficiary was Milton Holland, who attended the Albany Manual Labor Academy in Athens County. The academy, which accepted all races, had trained him as a shoemaker. When the war broke out, Holland was among those who attempted to volunteer. Failing, he took a position as a personal servant to Nelson H. Van Vorhees of the 3rd Ohio Volunteer Infantry Regiment. Holland used his time in the 3rd Ohio's camp to gain some practical experience in soldiering. He put this experience to good advantage; soon after mustering into the 127th Ohio Volunteer Infantry (OVI), he received a promotion to serve as the C Company first sergeant.[41]

In this respect, the USCT regiments were similar to the other Union volunteer regiments. Because members of volunteer units lacked any actual combat experience, they selected their leaders according to perceived abilities or social standing. Holland had demonstrated leadership by taking charge of a group of soldiers traveling to volunteer for the Massachusetts regiments. The group had camped in Athens when Holland met with Langston, who convinced him that he and his comrades should enlist in Ohio.

The physical descriptions of the 5th USCT soldiers indicate that they ranged from extremely light skinned or "white" to extremely dark skinned or "black," although the Regimental Muster Rolls list nearly half as black. Their heights varied from 4'10" to 6'4", with an average height of 5'7". They ranged in age from fifteen to fifty-five with an average age of slightly more than twenty-four.[42]

The youngest soldier, George Ivy, gave his age as eighteen when he enlisted during the last week of June, but his mother, apparently fearing the loss of her son, reported his true age, which was fourteen, to the recruiting officer. Governor Tod discharged him from the service in October.[43]

Mustering into the 127th OVI was similar to mustering into one of Ohio's white regiments.[44] The recruiting agents conducted a cursory medical examination to ensure that the men were physically able to perform as soldiers. This examination included making sure the soldier was able to bite well enough to open the cartridges for his rifle. The soldiers signed the enlistment contract if they were able. If a soldier could not sign his name, he made his mark and a person who could sign witnessed. The agent then provided the recruit with a pass that provided him with free transportation to the 5th USCT's mustering location at Camp Delaware in central Ohio.

At Camp Delaware, the recruit mustered into one of the regiment's ten companies. The mustering officer for the company entered the recruit's age, date and place of enlistment, and length of service. Initially, all the recruits for the 5th USCT enlisted for a three-year term. Those who joined the regiment after it was in the field served one-year enlistments. The first seven companies filled rapidly, and nine companies completed their training in time to embark for Virginia in November.

That these men served in numbers disproportionate to their population is clear. The 1860 Census indicates that the black male population between the age of fifteen and forty in Ohio was approximately 7,100. Federal records show that more than 5,900 African-American soldiers enlisted from Ohio, although the figure likely includes some soldiers who came from Kentucky and Indiana.[45] These men joined to fight for the future of their nation and the future of their race. They believed their service would have an impact on how they would fare in the years after the war. They responded to this belief by enlisting and encouraging others to enlist. These men offered themselves to serve under white officers. These black men knew that they would receive unequal treatment but were willing to fight in hopes that following generations would be able to achieve equality. Only the future would reveal whether the results of military service met the expectations of the African-American soldier. Was there, as Douglass claimed, "no power on earth which can deny that he has earned the right to citizenship in the United States"?

2

Leaders

THE UNITED STATES COLORED Troops was an experiment for the Union. While radical Republicans believed that the arming of blacks was essential to ensuring their eventual freedom, they also felt that the African-American soldiers should have the best leadership possible to ensure the success of the experiment. The racial and political climate of the 1860s dictated that the officers for the 5th USCT would be white. While there were people in Ohio who believed that blacks should not be slaves, few were so bold as to claim that blacks were the social and intellectual equals of whites. Additionally, an officer's commission was a coveted prize. Governors took advantage of the volunteer regiments to reward party faithfuls, to gain favor with powerful or influential families, and to acquire leverage in areas where their popularity was low. In 1863, Ohio's governor David Tod was no exception in his need to gain favor with his backers. Prospective officers of colored regiments were required to pass a qualifying examination, however, so the governor could not freely offer the posts.

The requests to command or to be an officer in Ohio's first black regiment predated the authority to raise such a regiment. Governor Tod received several offers from Ohioans eager to lead black soldiers. He also received offers from individuals interested in recruiting men for the regiment and from African-American citizens seeking to join the Union army. Governor Tod's response to the early requests was uniform: Ohio is not now raising colored troops. However, by June 1863, Governor Tod began to give more encouragement to applicants. He knew that Secretary of War Stanton would give Ohio permission to raise colored regiments once Massachusetts finished raising its levies.

Tod had an officer in mind to command the 127th Ohio Volunteer Infantry Regiment, but he also took the advice of prominent Ohio African Americans. Langston, who was active in several legal struggles for his race, was influential in the selection of the regiment's commander. He believed that Oberlin's Giles Waldo Shurtleff would be the best candidate for the command. Although Shurtleff was neither a Democrat nor politically powerful, he had the backing of several of the state's African-American leaders. Both Langston and Wall wrote to Shurtleff to persuade him to apply for the position. Langston also visited Tod to plead Shurtleff's case. Shurtleff was willing to take command but did not want to be involved in the political wrangling that he believed would be needed to secure the position.[1]

After Shurtleff had his interview with Governor Tod, he was impressed with the change in the governor. "The governor seems a different man from Governor Tod of last year. His interest is enlisted in behalf of the blacks and he is thoroughly in earnest in his efforts to support the administration in all its measures."[2] The opinion of the black soldiers, however, was the deciding factor between the governor's choice and those of the African-American leadership.

Because the army insisted on having fully qualified officers for the colored troops, Governor Tod was not able to simply appoint officers for the regiment. The prospective officers had to face a panel of regular army officers to prove their martial and mental prowess. The board that examined the candidates for the Ohio regiment met in Cincinnati from July to December. The Cincinnati board consisted of three regular army officers. While nearly all the candidates qualified for some level of commission, Governor Tod's choice for the colonelcy of the regiment failed to qualify for a colonel's commission.

Captain Lewis McCoy, the officer whom Governor Tod chose to command the regiment, was not equal to the task. Although McCoy was already a captain and a staff officer, his selection for the command of the colored regiment was political. His scores on his qualification examination showed him to be deficient in military tactics, and although he passed the other areas, he did not receive a "fully qualified" score in any area. His performance on the qualifying examination was only good enough to qualify him to continue in his rank as captain in the regiment, which he declined to do.[3]

The qualifying examination was a feature unique to the commissioning of officers for the USCT regiments. The army hoped to assure the Union leadership that if the USCT regiments performed poorly, it was not because of any fault in their officers. The test examined the officers in six areas: tactics, regulations, general military knowledge, math, history, and geography. It was possible to fail three of the six areas and still receive a commission, as did two of the 5th USCT's second lieutenants and a first lieutenant. Like any testing procedure, the qualifying examination was imperfect, and the impression that the officer made on the board members played a role, as did political considerations. Although McCoy received a captain's recommendation from the board, his scores were lower than those of four officers recommended for second lieutenant and lower than all but two of those men recommended for first lieutenant.[4]

The Cincinnati board showed the value of the War Department's decision to require examinations for the USCT's prospective officers. Without such an organization, Governor Tod would have been free to appoint Captain McCoy to the leadership of the regiment.

McCoy's scores on the examination reflected his own assessment of his skills. Shurtleff wrote that "Capt. M[cCoy] says he is not familiar with the details of military duty and should probably resign within a few months."[5] Despite this self-assessment and the board results, both McCoy and Tod continued to seek the appointment for McCoy. He remained in nominal command of the regiment throughout its recruitment and training.

Although McCoy lacked the military aptitude to lead the regiment, the men of the regiment liked him. When Tod visited the men in Camp Delaware near the end of July, he asked them who they would want as their regiment's commander. They requested Captain McCoy's appointment. When the regiment held its last formation at Camp Delaware before leaving for Virginia, the men presented Captain McCoy with a gold watch chain and gave his wife a gold ring as tokens of their esteem.[6]

The 5th USCT's first commander was Colonel James Conine of Middleport, Ohio. Colonel Conine came to the unit as a veteran officer, having previously served as a first lieutenant with the 1st Independent Battery of Kentucky Light Artillery and on the staff of General Jacob Cox, a prominent Ohio Democrat. His scores on the qualification examination were no better than those of some of the captains. He was "qualified" in military tactics and regulations, and received a "passing" mark in general military knowledge, math, history, and geography.[7] Once again, the qualifications of the officer played only a part in the commissioning process. He took command of the regiment after it had arrived in Virginia in late November.

Colonel Conine never developed the relationship with the men of the regiment that Lieutenant Colonel Shurtleff and Captain McCoy enjoyed. His background was significantly different from Shurtleff's or McCoy's. Conine had grown up in southern Ohio but had moved to Lexington, Kentucky, about sixty miles south of Cincinnati, as an adult. In Lexington, he had been the drill officer in John Hunt Morgan's rifle company. Most of his company mates held secessionist views, so it was a surprise to them when he decided to join those volunteering for the Union forces. The (Louisville) *Journal* found his later commission as the commander of the 5th USCT to be even more startling. That paper noted his commission with an explanation and sarcastic congratulation: "He is a Northern man by birth. We congratulate him upon the *proud* position to which he has been *elevated,* as the commander of a 'nigger' regiment."[8]

The lieutenant colonel of the regiment was Giles W. Shurtleff. The thirty-two-year-old Shurtleff had been born in Canada but had lived in Oberlin most of his life. When the war broke out, Shurtleff and many of his Oberlin classmates formed a company of the 7th Ohio Volunteer Infantry. His company elected him to be the captain, and he led them in both drill and prayers. At 5'9", he was not an imposing figure, but he had a commanding presence. His brief command of Company C, 7th OVI, ended when he was captured by Confederates at Keesler's Cross Lanes, Virginia, in July 1861. He remained a prisoner for thirteen months, spending time in Richmond's Libby Prison, in Salisbury, North Carolina, and in three different prisons in South Carolina before being exchanged.

After returning to Oberlin, he resumed his studies at Oberlin College and decided to enter the ministry. Like many Oberlin College students, Shurtleff held strong antislavery and religious beliefs. Even before Governor Tod announced the formation of an Ohio colored regiment, Shurtleff wrote,

> I rejoice to learn how thoroughly the cruel hatred of the black race is being dispelled. I regard the movement in this direction

as by far the most encouraging aspect of the war. God bless the negroes and make them wise and prudent in this time of their great deliverance. If I were going to the field, I should feel tempted to ask for command of colored troops.[9]

However, Shurtleff was not inclined to go to the field because he was near completion of his studies at Oberlin and had already begun to give sermons in Congregationalist churches around the state. Only a plea from Langston and Wall persuaded Shurtleff to seek command. Even so, he wrote, "I do not care for the position for my own sake. I prefer to continue my preparation of my cherished work [the ministry] and to hasten the day when I can . . . enjoy all the blessings of [that work]. But if God can use me for the greater good in the field, . . . I ought to go."[10] On July 29, 1863, Governor Tod appointed him to be the regiment's second in command. Despite his knowledge of the regiment and high scores on the qualifying examination, his lack of political ties and his several confrontations with Governor Tod over Captain McCoy's qualifications prevented him from receiving the appointment to command the regiment.

The 5th USCT had authorization for nine officers in the regimental headquarters. Four of these officers were the regimental commander, the lieutenant colonel, the major, and the adjutant. These officers had the same requirements for command of colored troops as any of the company officers. The regiment's other staff officers, the surgeon, his two assistants, the quartermaster, and the chaplain, did not have to take the qualifying examination. Still, the regiment never had a full complement of staff officers. The regiment was without a surgeon until May 22, 1864, when Lyman Allen, one of the two assistant surgeons, received a promotion to fill the position. The regiment never received another assistant surgeon, despite the persistent requests of its commanders. The chaplain's position went unfilled until October 29, 1865.[11]

Part of the difficulty in filling staff positions resulted from the lack of qualified applicants for the positions. However, in the case of the chaplain, the difficulty lay elsewhere. The first applicant was the Reverend John Cowles, the son of Oberlin professor Henry Cowles. He applied for the position in early January 1864, but the officers could not agree on the Congregationalist minister. Since chaplains could only be appointed with the unanimous consent of a regiment's officers, Cowles did not receive a commission. Shurtleff had mixed feelings about Cowles's qualifications. He wrote, "I do not think he is exactly adapted for the place, but doubt whether we shall do better. He is talented, a fine speaker and will be quite an addition to our staff, but I fear he will not be a practical worker among the *men*."[12]

The second applicant for the chaplaincy was James R. Brown, a Presbyterian minister from Perry, Illinois. Brown had a commission from General Butler, the necessary certificate from five ministers stating that he was a minister of the church in good standing, and had been duly elected by the officers of the 5th USCT.

However, even though his appointment was dated May 29, 1864, he did not arrive in the regiment until June 5. The strength of the regiment was 35 officers and 785 enlisted men. But by the time Brown's muster was possible, the regiment's strength had dropped to 34 officers and 775 enlisted men—below the minimum required strength of 35 officers and 780 enlisted men established by Congress in 1861. Because the regiment no longer met the personnel requirements for a chaplain's assignment, the muster was disallowed, and Brown returned to Illinois on August 4.[13]

The regiment finally filled the chaplain position on October 29, 1864, when the officers voted to accept the Reverend James L. Patton, a Congregationalist minister and Oberlin College graduate. Patton had previously gained some brief notoriety for his part in the Oberlin-Wellington Rescue.[14]

The surgeon's position was filled, not through the acceptance of a qualified surgeon, but through the promotion of an unqualified assistant surgeon. Lyman Allen, of Vernon, Ohio, had been a hospital steward before accepting a commission to join the 5th USCT. He did not have any formal training in medicine but passed a medical review board in March 1864. In November 1864, he faced court martial charges for "Gross Neglect of Duty, Failure to Obey Orders, and Gross Inhumanity." He was convicted only of neglect, which cost him one month's pay but allowed him to continue as the regimental surgeon.

The charges stemmed from an incident in late September 1864. Shurtleff had ordered Allen to tend to a soldier whose foot had been partially torn off by a piece of flying shrapnel. Allen ignored the order because he believed that "a man with a part of his foot cut off by a piece of shell was not suffering much pain."[15]

Allen continued to serve as the regiment's surgeon until his discharge for refusing to face a medical review board in April 1865. Shurtleff requested that Allen be sent before the board because Shurtleff believed "that he is wholly incompetent and that the efficiency of this regiment demands that he be removed and a competent medical officer assigned." Upon being summoned to the board, Allen tendered his resignation.[16]

The final member of the staff was the regimental quartermaster, James B. F. Marsh. Marsh entered the regiment from Oberlin College. He felt strongly that he was called to "work in some way for the elevation of the black race" by "identifying [himself] with black soldiers fighting *with* them and *for* them."[17] Marsh, who found the time to be married while on sick leave, left the service soon after the end of the hostilities but served faithfully until his resignation was accepted in May 1865.

Several officers in the regiment accepted a commission for a rank lower than that for which they had qualified, because they chose to enter active service with the regiment rather than wait for the recruitment of the second Ohio African-American regiment. Seven officers qualified for commissions as major. Only Ira Terry actually received this commission. The other six officers accepted posts as company commanders. The remaining four commanders had qualified as captains, as did Captain McCoy, who declined his USCT commission.

Nearly all of the ten original company commanders had previous service in volunteer regiments. Except for the Ford brothers, Ellery and Frank, who commanded companies F and I, and Charles Oren, who commanded Company E, the commanders had more than a year in service before entering the USCT. Oren was the only commander in the regiment who had not already served in the army. Despite their general lack of experience, these officers proved to be good commanders. Two of them—Company A's Orlando Brockway and Company E's Charles Oren—died leading their men into combat in June 1864.

The most successful of the regiment's officers, Captain Ellery Ford, rose from commanding Company F to become a brevet brigadier general while serving as commander of the 107th USCT.[18]

The regiment's company commanders also included three officers whose judgment and character were questionable. The examining board did not conduct background investigations, so the board members had no indication whether these officers had a history of misbehavior. Their selection for commission and subsequently as company commanders indicate that they had gained the confidence of their superior officers. Only the course of events would show the deficiency of these men. One such officer was Captain Calvin Spear, the Company K commander. He deserted the regiment while it was serving in the trenches in front of Petersburg, Virginia. Colonel Conine wrote a statement about Spear's utter worthlessness as an officer and his cowardice in the face of the enemy to Department Headquarters. Conine also accused Spear of disrespect and of cheating his soldiers by selling them worthless equipment, and concluded that Spear was "an adventurer, a dishonest speculator, unworthy to associate with gentlemen and wholly unfit for the responsible position he occupied."[19] The army dismissed Spear from the service.

Surprisingly, Captain Karl Von Heintze, the Company B commander, also was dismissed from the service. His record before joining the regiment was good. He had graduated from Berlin's Kriegsakademie, served as an officer in the Prussian army, and had a captain's commission in the 108th Ohio Volunteer Infantry Regiment. Every indicator pointed to a successful command. He had impressed the examining board well enough to earn a recommendation for a major's commission. In May 1864, he wrote to General Butler, asking for a major's position in one of the newly forming USCT regiments. Butler did not respond to the request.

Von Heintze had gained a reputation for lacking leadership abilities. Major Terry, who was in temporary command of the regiment, noted that Von Heintze was

> totally unfit to have charge of a body of men as he is habitually negligent of them . . . he has never been able to do duty when the emergency demanded character, decision and determination . . . has never started on a march without falling out upon it . . . has never heard that a battle was imminent without evincing a physical weakness entirely unbecoming an officer. . . . As a company accountant he is good for nothing. As a disciplinarian and drillmaster he is the same.[20]

In the June attack on Richmond, Von Heintze became prostrate with fear. His soldiers had to carry him from the field, apparently paralyzed, but with no wounds. The forty-three-year-old graduate of the Prussian Kriegsakademie simply would fight no longer. Lyman Allen, the regiment's surgeon, commented that "[Von Heintze], on the only occasion when he was with the Regt under fire, was brought to me on a stretcher, unable to stand, or to converse with common reason, while his sudden illness and rapid recovery made it probable that his sickness was the effect on his nerves of the excitement of the battle."[21] At forty-three, Von Heintze was the oldest officer in the regiment. It is possible that the hard campaigning of the winter months had sapped his will to fight. It is also possible that the disappointment of not receiving a higher commission than his previous rank soured him on command. Whatever the reason, Von Heintze did not measure up to the standards of his fellow USCT officers.

Another of the commanders who did not measure up was Captain Gustave Fahrion. Fahrion was a good combat leader, but he was dishonest. What made Fahrion an interesting figure is that his superior officers knew about his character but allowed him to continue in service. There are several examples of Fahrion's dishonesty and his superiors' awareness of this dishonest behavior.

In November 1863, Captain Fahrion became aware that some enlisted soldiers had robbed two widows living at London Bridge, Virginia. His company took up a collection to help the widows with their living expenses. The brigade commander, Colonel Alonzo Draper, contributed seven dollars to the collection, giving the money to Captain Fahrion. The soldiers also gave the money they collected for the widows to Captain Fahrion. But Fahrion never paid the money to the women. He compounded this error, in Colonel Draper's eyes, by asking for the colonel's assistance in getting one of the other officers in the brigade to make good on a debt he owed to a friend of Captain Fahrion's. Draper commented that Captain Fahrion's moral theory was superior to his practice.[22]

By the summer of 1864, the regiment was in a brigade commanded by Colonel Samuel Duncan. Captain Fahrion's machinations were equally apparent to Colonel Duncan. In late July, Colonel Conine and Major Terry were both away sick. Lieutenant Colonel Shurtleff believed that he had to be careful of his health because "Capt. Fahrion would be the senior officer in [his] absence." However, Colonel Duncan assured Shurtleff that if none of the field grade officers were available for service, he would appoint one temporarily rather than allow Fahrion to take command of the regiment. When Captain Fahrion attempted to resign his commission that fall in hopes of gaining a major's billet in one of the newly forming Ohio volunteer regiments, Colonel Shurtleff approved the action, hoping to rid his regiment of Captain Fahrion, who "[was] the ranking captain in the regiment, [but] the last officer that any of his superiors who have known him would trust with responsibility." General Charles Paine, the division commander, agreed with Colonel Shurtleff's assessment.[23] Despite these officers' endorsements, General John Gibbon, the corps commander, refused to accept Captain Fahrion's resignation.

In October 1864, Fahrion faced court-martial charges for improperly borrowing money from his soldiers and for collecting the pay of soldiers who had died. His good conduct in battle helped him, and the tribunal allowed him to stay in the service after he repaid the money he had taken.[24]

This proved to be the second occasion in which Captain Fahrion had avoided being dismissed from the service. Before serving with the 5th USCT, Fahrion had been a first lieutenant with the 67th Ohio Volunteer Infantry. He had been on duty as officer of the day on Christmas Eve in 1861. His commanding officer's report noted that he had found Lieutenant Fahrion drunk on duty. He told Fahrion that if Fahrion resigned his commission immediately, the colonel or regimental commander would not bring charges against him. Fahrion accepted the offer and left the service three weeks later.[25]

Of the fifty-seven officers who served with the regiment, twenty-six remained to muster out with the unit in September 1865 (see appendix C). Six died in service, four received wounds so severe that they had to be discharged, three were dismissed from the service, and three accepted promotions to serve in other USCT regiments. The other fifteen officers, including Colonel Shurtleff, resigned for personal reasons.

The officers who led the 5th USCT were a diverse group. They had different reasons for wanting to command colored troops. Some of these men had strong abolitionist ideals, some had powerful political connections, others simply wanted to be officers regardless of the complexion of their men. While their individual ideologies may have motivated their service, nearly all of them served well and faithfully.

3

Training a Regiment for War

G ETTING MEN INTO THE service was a task that the leadership of the African-American community and politicians could accomplish. The task of turning those men into soldiers would fall into the hands of military men. As in other Civil War units, the officers of the 5th USCT had to train their new charges. They had to instill an unquestioning obedience and a sense of discipline, and teach the men the drill necessary to make them an effective fighting force. The fact of the men's enlistment showed that they believed themselves able to become soldiers; it was up to the officers to realize that potential.

At Camp Delaware, twenty-five miles north of Columbus, in central Ohio, the recruits learned the fundamentals of their military role. The 5th USCT remained at Camp Delaware until November 1863, using the time to drill, to practice with firearms, and to become accustomed to camp life. This period of training presented a new experience for the soldiers. While many of the men were accustomed to long days of hard labor, the imposed discipline would have been new to all but those who had been enslaved. After the sergeants and officers learned their drill, they controlled the soldiers' time from 5:00 A.M. to 9:30 P.M.

The day started with an hour of squad drill under the direction of the noncommissioned officers. Following drill, the soldiers ate breakfast and policed the camp. Although the germ theory of medicine had not achieved wide acceptance, observation through the early years of the war showed that clean camps reduced sickness among soldiers. Whether the soldiers were aware of this or not, their attention to camp police earned them a reputation for upright behavior and for cleanliness. Their behavior encouraged a Columbus newspaper to comment, "So far, they have conducted themselves in a highly creditable manner" and "have gained a good reputation in the neighborhood of their camp for honesty, sobriety, and general good behavior; and have also the praise of their officers for obedience and attention to discipline."[1] Lieutenant Colonel Shurtleff commented that the "boys have a real soldierly pride."[2]

After breakfast, selected soldiers practiced guarding the encampment while the remainder performed company drill. During the hour before the noon meal, NCOs participated in a "School of the NCO" that taught them their basic tasks and duties. Although it is not clear who instructed the sergeants at Camp Delaware, Major Ira Terry, who took command of the 22nd USCT in October 1864, had responsibility for the training after the regiment transferred to Virginia. This training continued throughout the war; later the sergeants received training in the field artillery manual.

The regiment spent the remainder of the day in battalion drill and ended its training with an evening dress parade and retreat. The retreat call, which meant that the soldier was to be in his bed, was at 9:30 P.M.[3]

The long hours devoted to drill reflect the tactics of the day. Because of the relatively poor accuracy of individual weapons, armies developed mass-fire tactics to increase their effective firepower. Soldiers had to learn to march in step, load their weapons, fire, reload, and move from place to place on the battlefield as a member of a unit. The only time that the men would operate semi-independently was when deployed as skirmishers.

The regiment's training was rigorous, but the officers still had time to keep abreast of news from the war. The newspaper reports that the Confederates had offered a reward for the scalps of black soldiers and their white officers caused a stir in camp. Shurtleff dismissed the report as ridiculous but took the rumor as further proof of the rightness of his cause.[4]

A glaring deficiency in the 5th USCT's training was the lack of regimental drill. The tactics of the day called for commanders to maneuver regiments as a unit. Those units that could not perform as a regiment were of little value to their higher commanders. Unfortunately for the 5th USCT, it did not even have a regimental commander to organize such training at Camp Delaware. Captain McCoy, who was in nominal command of the regiment, did very little actual training with the unit, choosing to spend much of his time away from camp after failing his qualifying exam. Shurtleff assumed the duties of regimental drillmaster and was very pleased with his success, but he did not have the experience needed to conduct a full regiment drill.

Initially, the men lacked discipline and the officers were careless with the account and record books. Shurtleff published orders setting forth the drill schedule and personally supervised the bookkeeping tasks. He had confidence in the men, noting, "From a mob, they have grown to be orderly, well drilled soldiers. [The men] drill six hours each day. I never saw men learn faster. If efficiently commanded, ours will be as good a regiment as has left the state."[5]

Shurtleff hit upon a key factor in the soldiers' attention to their duties. He realized that they appreciated the "sublime truth that they are making character for a whole race."[6] The soldiers' letters show that they also believed this truth. In a letter to his sister, Joel Spears wrote, "Tell the ladies of Pomeroy that we will not disgrace ourselves by the mere act of cowardice . . . tell the boys not to stay in Pomeroy like cowards but come to the bloody field and show there [sic] manhood."[7]

As the men adjusted to their duties, the officers also adjusted to the realities of their new responsibilities. McCoy's absence left Shurtleff free to imprint the regiment with his distinctive ideologies. One of the hardest of the new rules for the officers and the soldiers was the colonel's stand against profanity. While nearly half of the officers in camp by September were "professors of religion," it still was not until October that Shurtleff was satisfied with the reformation of some officers.[8]

The soldiers and officers of the 5th USCT showed marked improvement over the early weeks of fall, but the regiment still lacked weapons, several lieutenants, surgeons, and a chaplain. Lieutenant Colonel Shurtleff wrote a letter to Governor Tod protesting the missing items.[9] The governor promised to do what he could. The lack of serviceable weapons was not unique to the colored troops. A general shortage of weapons was a normal situation for units that had not received orders to deploy to the theater of operations.

The unique difficulty faced by colored troops was that while the regiment had noncommissioned officers who would very likely have been capable of performing the duties of lieutenants, no African Americans received consideration for these positions. In white

Union regiments, most officers came from within the regiment. Lieutenants and captains often were elected by the men of the unit. Without this ready source of experienced leadership, the colored regiments had to rely on the ability of the examining boards to weed out the poor officers. They soon learned what a weak reed such a reliance was.

It was still September when the regiment dismissed its first officer. Second Lieutenant Thurston Owens, who received a commission from the Cincinnati examining board, was incapable of handling his liquor. He created a disturbance at Camp Delaware. On Shurtleff's recommendation, Governor Tod dismissed him from the service.[10]

The absence of surgeons hampered the development of the green regiment. Fifteen soldiers died from pneumonia, smallpox, and other sicknesses at Camp Delaware. Near the end of September, there were more than thirty cases of measles in the camp, and still no surgeon. Shurtleff complained that the camp hospital was poorly supplied and that the men were not getting the treatment they deserved. His visit to the surgeon general's headquarters brought some relief in the appointment of an assistant surgeon on September 21. The regiment received its second assistant surgeon when Lyman Allen received a promotion from quartermaster sergeant of the 41st OVI to fill the position.[11]

The African-American community took pride in its regiment. On August 4, 1863, a special train brought six carloads filled with family members and well-wishers, who brought large quantities of food to the soldiers at Camp Delaware. The grateful soldiers gladly took a break from their rigorous training to share a picnic with their visitors. This visit was a tangible symbol of the African-American community's support of its soldiers.

Ohio's African-American community also chose a more lasting symbol of its pride in its soldiers, paying $175 to provide regimental colors and the color company (C Company) guidons. Governor Tod presented the colors, inscribed with "Victory or Death," to the regiment on a rainy November day, immediately before the regiment departed for Fort Monroe, Virginia. Former governor William Dennison accepted the colors for the regiment, saying he "felt confident that they would never be disgraced by those into whose charge they were placed . . . though they may come back torn and tattered from use, they would never be tarnished."[12] As governor, Dennison had rejected African-American participation in the war, but as a private citizen, he was an avid supporter of the black troops.

Governor Tod's assessment of the day's events indicated a recognition of the special situation facing the African-American soldiers. He said, "There were many men, and abolitionists among them who never had the least expectation of seeing a large portion of the colored men of Ohio formed into an orderly, well-drilled, and in every respect, an efficient regiment." He complimented the men on their conduct at Camp Delaware, noting that it had been superior to that of many other regiments, and warned them that while he would do what he could to remove their burdens, they would likely continue to labor under adverse conditions.[13]

4

The Regiment Moves South

GOVERNOR TOD'S REMARKS PROVED correct. The prejudice of some in the army immediately created unpleasantness. The regiment traveled by train to Baltimore, then took a steamer south on Chesapeake Bay. Upon arrival in Virginia, the 5th USCT received assignment to the XVIII Corps' African Brigade and took up quarters at an entrenched camp near Norfolk. The regiment shared this camp with a detachment from the 7th New York Artillery Battery, which was a white unit under the command of Lieutenant Martin V. McIntyre.

Brigadier General Edward Wild, the African Brigade commander and commanding officer of the troops posted in the Norfolk and Portsmouth areas, placed Colonel Conine in charge of the camp, but Lieutenant McIntyre refused to take orders from the commander of a USCT regiment. The New Yorkers had not shared the duties of guarding and maintaining the camp, but what was more important, the lieutenant and his wife occupied a house that the camp needed for a hospital. Despite Colonel Conine's seniority, it took intervention by General Wild to secure the cooperation of the New York unit.[1] McIntyre's behavior, while an isolated incident, brings to light the sort of occurrence that could only have faced the Colored Troops regiments.

The 5th USCT initiated a pattern of encampment at Norfolk that it would follow as often as possible for the remainder of the regiment's service. The regiment initially drew wall tents for the officers and shelter tents for the men. Lieutenant Colonel Shurtleff believed this was inadequate housing for the men and set out to correct the deficiency. Within a week, the men were at work building log huts with brick fireplaces. They cut wood, but much of their building

32

material came from ruined homes in Norfolk and from abandoned Confederate camps.[2]

The black soldiers engaged rebels soon after the regiment arrived in Virginia. Two companies under the command of Major Terry accompanied a cavalry unit on a three-day sweep through Princess Ann County. This force captured eight guerrillas and 150 horses and liberated five hundred slaves.[3]

The 5th USCT's initial missions called for hard campaigning in Virginia's Tidewater region and the swamps of northern North Carolina. The raids were part of General Butler's attempt to separate the rebel guerrillas from their civilian base, free slaves to deny their labor to the Confederacy, and destroy as many of the Confederates' supplies as possible. The soldiers, hunting guerrillas, traversed the swamps for most of December. Sergeant Holland noted that the soldiers campaigned without overcoats or blankets. Fortunately for the Ohioans, the weather, while cool, was dry.[4]

The Union's African-American soldiers quickly learned that the government did not care about the state of their equipment—unless the soldiers lost it. Confederate guerrillas captured Private James Corne, a thirty-four-year-old farmer from Athens, during one of the skirmishes. His service record, which gives no mention of his fate, merely notes that should he return from captivity, he owed the government for the loss of his weapon.[5]

Colonel Conine took the regiment on a raid through the Great Dismal Swamp toward Elizabeth City, North Carolina. This raid shared the objectives of the other raids, but General Butler believed that the larger force would encourage the inhabitants of northern North Carolina to declare their allegiance to the Union.

The raid had its enemies—on both sides. Before departing for North Carolina, General Wild sent a dispatch to General George Getty alerting him that there would be an influx of contrabands. Wild ended the message by warning Getty that if the contrabands were obstructed in any way, that the obstructer would be severely punished. Getty took offense at the tone of Wild's message but assured him that he had always assisted colored persons as much as possible. However, less than a week into the expedition, Wild sent a dispatch to General Butler complaining that cavalrymen from Getty's cavalry brigade had been sent out "in advance to warn the inhabitants that 'nigger-stealers' were coming to plunder them of everything."[6]

Confederate General George Pickett suggested that the best course of action would be to take the slaves farther south, out of range of Northern troops. He believed that the December raid was an extension of Washington policy regarding the raising of African-American troops. He regarded the freeing of slaves and other property an "outrage." Although he lacked sufficient forces to stop the incursion, he suggested that "against such warfare there is but one resource—to hang at once every one captured belonging to the expedition, and afterward any one caught who belongs to Butler's department."[7]

The force, which consisted of soldiers from the 1st USCT, 2nd North Carolina Volunteer, 1st North Carolina Volunteer, and 55th Massachusetts Volunteer Infantry Regiments as well as two cavalry companies from the 5th and 11th Pennsylvania Cavalry Regiments, was under the direct command of General Wild. The troops from the 5th USCT left the entrenched camp on December 5 and marched into the swamps. The column met little resistance from the guerrillas except for one brief encounter in which they killed thirteen rebels. Lieutenant Colonel Shurtleff's column captured a guerrilla. General Butler questioned the man and, after a drumhead court-martial, had him hanged.[8]

The four companies of the regiment patrolling under the command of G Company's Captain George Cock had the toughest fight. The Confederates opened fire from a distance of four hundred yards, killing three Union soldiers with their initial volley. Captain Cock ordered the Ohioans to return fire from prone positions, then organized the companies into flanking elements that drove the guerrillas into flight. Cock's report commended the men's behavior under fire.[9]

Difficult as the time in the marshes proved to be, it had a positive effect on the white soldiers of the XVIII Corps. The African Americans proved good soldiers, standing firm in skirmishes with the guerrillas, taking prisoners, and destroying camps. The accompanying cavalrymen said, "No soldiers have ever done as hard marching through swamps and marshes as cheerfully as [the African-American soldiers] did, and that if [the cavalry] had to follow [the African-American soldiers] for any length of time, it would kill their horses."[10]

While the division's cavalrymen showed newfound respect for the 5th USCT, the raid also served to strengthen Lieutenant Colonel

Shurtleff's resolve to aid his men in their quest to end slavery. Shurtleff's writings show him to have been a man who had sincere concerns for the welfare of the black race, but he still was shocked at the condition of the contrabands that the regiment liberated in its December raids. The firsthand encounter with the "brutalizing effects of slavery" made him resolve to give his life to end slavery. His main concern became that the war would end before the South could "be driven to recognize in the Black a man, a *soldier* and a *man.*" Shurtleff intended to continue training the troops to make them as good a regiment as he knew how. While he believed they already were a good unit, he wanted them to become one of the best in the service.[11]

The regiment still needed more discipline and training to make it an effective unit. The new year brought a brief lull in the 5th USCT's combat duties, but the inactivity strained the patience of the officers. The regiment settled into the tedium of winter quarters, and the soldiers faced new challenges to their discipline. The regimental logs show that the soldiers committed at least twenty-one minor offenses between January and April. The offenses included disobedience to orders, failure to perform duties, fighting, profanity, and theft. Initially, Colonel Conine restrained his punishments to fines of up to ten dollars and manual labor, which consisted of providing the camp with four to thirty cords of wood. For corporals and sergeants, the punishment always included loss of rank.

The first severe punishment recorded was twelve hours on an elevated bar, a form of corporal punishment. The soldier that received the punishment had to sit astride a four-inch-wide bar that was elevated about eight feet. This placed all of the soldier's weight on the base of his pelvis. Private Thomas Jenkins of Company A merited this punishment for his persistent disobedience of orders. Apparently, the punishment was successful, for Jenkins served without further difficulty.[12] Other corporal punishments included bucking and spread-eagling the soldiers, although the commander did not commonly use either punishment.

Soon after the regiment completed building the log houses for the men, the regiment received orders transferring it to Yorktown. Although Colonel Conine was annoyed at having to leave newly built quarters to some other unit, he was more annoyed because the orders were intended for the 2nd North Carolina Colored Volunteer

Regiment. That regiment's commander had more influence with General Butler than did the newly arrived Ohioans and was able to persuade the general to give the assignment to another regiment, since his regiment had settled in for the winter.

The monotony of winter quarters also brought out the worst in some of the officers. Colonel Conine dismissed two lieutenants and arrested Captain Spear for corrupt behavior. Although Conine took his responsibilities as an officer in the USCT seriously, one incident reveals that he was still very much a product of his society. The April muster roll shows that the army withheld $60.18 of the commander's pay for employing an enlisted man as a personal servant for ninety-five days.[13]

In addition to seeking improvement in the regiment's training, Lieutenant Colonel Shurtleff concerned himself with the men's spiritual well-being. He wrote to Oberlin seeking a suitable candidate for the chaplain's position. The Reverend John Cowles, whose father was a professor at Oberlin, applied for the post. Lieutenant Colonel Shurtleff wanted a chaplain badly, but felt that Reverend Cowles would not be the ideal choice for the regiment's men. He was, however, alone in this concern among the field grade officers. He wrote that Colonel Conine and Major Terry were both thoughtless concerning the moral and religious interests of the regiment. This belief that the regiment's leadership was irreligious led him to wonder that "men so openly profane and wicked can work for God and humanity."[14]

Besides the monotony facing the men and their officers, the chief concern over the winter was filling the ranks. The regiment left Ohio with only eighty soldiers in each company. They planned to complete their manning with contrabands so that they would have men in the regiment who were familiar with the area. Unfortunately, the Ohio regiment did not enlist the contrabands they had hoped; other units had already heavily recruited in the area. Compounding the difficulty was the raising in Ohio of the 27th USCT. Governor Tod would not allow the 5th USCT to recruit more soldiers there until that regiment filled its ranks. Colonel Conine sought permission to recruit soldiers in the Washington, D.C., and Baltimore areas, but did not receive this authorization from the Colored Troops Bureau.[15] Only in August, after the 27th USCT completed its recruiting, would the 5th USCT reach full strength.

The move to Yorktown consolidated the 2nd Brigade under the command of Colonel Samuel Duncan. The brigade comprised the 5th (Ohio), the 4th (Maryland), and 6th (western Pennsylvania) USCT Regiments. These units were part of the Department of Virginia and North Carolina, commanded by Major General Ben Butler. The two infantry brigades, one cavalry brigade, and one artillery brigade at Yorktown were all under the command of Brigadier General Isaac Wistar.

After its move to Yorktown, the regiment joined its brigade in a number of small raids to control Confederate guerrillas. The brigade was also involved in an audaciously planned raid on Richmond in early February. The Kilpatrick-Dahlgren raid, as it came to be known, took place between February 5 and February 9 and had as its purpose the destruction of Confederate supplies, the burning of the Tredegar Iron Works, the release of Union prisoners of war, and the capture of Jefferson Davis and his cabinet. The plan called for the Union cavalry to sweep the Confederate pickets from the road between Williamsburg and Richmond, bypass any serious opposition, and seize the Bottom Bridge, some eighteen miles east of Richmond.

The plan was a dismal failure. The cavalry failed to capture the Confederate pickets. By the time the seven infantry regiments passed over the same road, the Confederates sent up signal rockets to mark the approach in the Union soldiers. The cavalry also met stiff opposition at the bridge and was unable to dislodge the rebel force. Although the infantry marched 44 miles in a day, the raid failed, and they had to retrace their route. In all, the 5th USCT marched 110 miles in five days, each soldier carrying six days' rations and seventy rounds of ammunition in addition to his overcoat, blanket, and shelter half. Lieutenant Colonel Shurtleff boasted that his regiment did not leave a single straggler, while the New Yorkers left more than five hundred.[16]

March saw the regiment involved in nearly continuous patrolling. On the night of March 1, the 5th USCT began a march that would cover forty-four miles in twenty-three hours, including several hours in a rainstorm. The purpose of the march was to fix the rebel defenders while General Judson Kilpatrick and the 3rd Division, Cavalry Corps, raided the Confederate positions near Richmond. The returning cavalry force passed the infantrymen near New Kent

Court House. Since there was no further need for the diversion, the African-American troops reversed their march and returned to camp on March 5. During this march, Lieutenant Joseph Scroggs of H Company noticed that the civilian populace stayed indoors while the colored regiments marched through their midst. He attributed this to a fear on the part of the former slaveowners.[17] Scroggs's observation points out a popular misconception: that the USCT regiments were all composed of former slaves. In reality, the civilians had little more to fear from black Union soldiers than from white Union soldiers. There are no recorded incidents of soldiers from the 5th USCT engaging in any actions against civilians other than the liberation of slaves.

Immediately upon their return to Yorktown, the 5th USCT received orders to reprovision and prepare to board steamers. The steamers took the regiment as far as Portsmouth. From there, the 5th USCT took open rail cars to Suffolk, on the northern edge of the Great Dismal Swamp. The regiment's new duty was to protect the rail line and a government farm from an anticipated cavalry raid. The rebel force did not attack, so the regiment took advantage of the guard duty to get a much needed rest.

It was fortunate for the men that they had this rest, for when they returned to Yorktown, they did not even disembark but immediately set out with General Kilpatrick's cavalry on a raid against the north side of Richmond. General Wistar planned the expedition of March 9–10 as a trap for the Confederates, but the Union cavalry did not follow orders, and the Confederate infantry escaped before the Union infantry arrived. Again the 5th USCT did more marching than fighting, marching more than thirty miles without engaging the enemy. An expedition two days later netted forty Confederate prisoners.[18]

As the regiment marched through the month, the 38th Congress was debating the issue of black soldiers' pay. African-American soldiers entered the army under the terms of the Militia Act of July 17, 1862, which authorized the enlistment of blacks into the Union army at a rate of ten dollars per month, the same as government contract laborers earned. This meant that African-American privates earned three dollars less each month than did their white counterparts. For other ranks, the pay differential was much larger. Since black sergeants received the same pay as black privates, they received eleven dollars less a month than their white counterparts, or less than half their pay.[19]

The pay problem cut both ways. The soldiers realized that the unequal pay was another instance that showed that racial equality had not arrived. Low pay also made it difficult for the soldier to provide support for his family. In many cases, the pay that the soldier received as a private was not as much as he would have been earning at home; for those who had labored on family farms, their pay would not hire a replacement. Even so, the soldiers of the 5th USCT seemed more pragmatic about the pay issue than their comrades from the Massachusetts regiments. The difference was almost certainly one of timing. The soldiers who enlisted in the Ohio regiment believed they would be receiving less pay when they enlisted, while those who had enlisted in Massachusetts believed they would enlist under equal pay and bounty.

Some African-American soldiers felt that the commotion over pay demeaned their efforts in uniform by making it seem that they were excessively interested in pay and not interested enough in duty. One soldier in the 5th USCT, who wrote to the *Christian Recorder* under the pseudonym "Wild Jack," observed that the paymasters were ahead of Congress in paying out the black regiments. He said that the 5th USCT soldiers had received thirteen dollars a month from January 1864 through April 1864 and sixteen dollars a month thereafter. Wild Jack contended, "To hear a regiment all the time after money, goes to show that they only came after money; but a regiment who keeps her grievances to herself is more to my eyes, and I believe, to the public, the most thought of."[20]

Lieutenant Scroggs, on the other hand, felt that the unequal pay not only slighted the African-American soldiers but also undermined the work that he was doing on their behalf. He wrote in his diary,

> The rebels have not yet recognized or treated such colored soldiers as have fallen into their hands as prisoners of war, but have butchered, starved and even burnt them to death. Yet to these men, who voluntarily brave these dangers, our government pays but the poor pittance of $4 27/100 per [month.] Should this Congress adjourn without doing full and complete Justice to the *free colored volunteer* it will deserve that "perfidious" be attached to its number in history. I did not enter this service from any mercenary motive but to assist in removing the unreasonable prejudice against the colored race, and to contribute

a share however small toward making the negro an effective
instrument in crushing out this unholy rebellion.[21]

Scroggs intended to submit his resignation in protest of the Congressional inaction. However, the Senate and then the House agreed
to rectify the pay inequity, thereby removing one of the barriers to
political and legal equality facing African Americans.[22]

Equal treatment by the Confederacy remained a problematic
issue for the black soldiers and their officers. On April 17, 1864,
the regiment received news of the Fort Pillow massacre. Lieutenant
Colonel Shurtleff wrote, "The government *must* notice this brutal-
ity. If it does not, it seems to me that the only course for black
soldiers is to resort to the black flag. Show no quarter." Earlier in
the war, he had hastened to reassure Mary Burton that reports of
Confederate atrocities against African-American soldiers and their
commanders were absurd. The massacre cleared any doubts he may
have had on that score.[23]

The regiment redoubled its training after the news of the Fort
Pillow massacre. The men replaced worn equipment, drilled in
skirmishing tactics, and practiced marksmanship. The regiment
expected the worst from the Confederates but worked to be the
best they could become. Shurtleff prepared the men for movement
toward Richmond. He believed that they would be involved in another peninsula campaign.[24]

Reorganization of the department in April united six USCT regiments into the two brigades of the "colored division." This organization placed them outside the ordinary scheme, removing
them from the XVIII Corps. This was the first time they were under the command of a general who commanded only USCT units.
The records show no reason for the reorganization, but it did not
affect all the department's USCT regiments. Seven of the eight
other USCT regiments remained brigaded with white units.[25] Lieutenant Colonel Shurtleff feared the move indicated that General
Ulysses S. Grant intended to pursue a policy of keeping the African-
American soldiers on garrison and fatigue duty. He felt this would
be harmful to his men's quest for equality and argued that although such duty would protect the soldiers, it would not force
the Confederates to acknowledge the African Americans as soldiers
and men.[26]

Shurtleff's concern touched the heart of the blacks' service. For the service to have meaning, the men had to serve honorably and fight well. They could serve honorably no matter what the circumstance, but they were dependent on their commanders to place them on the battlefield. Fortunately for the Ohioans, their commanders would do just that. Whatever the reason for assigning the USCTs into a colored division, it was temporary. When the 5th USCT deployed to City Point to join the forces arrayed against Petersburg, the organizational table showed them as part of the 3rd Division, XVIII Corps. Except for the addition of two batteries from the New York Light Artillery, this division contained the same troops that had briefly borne the colored division title.[27]

At City Point, the regiment began more severe duty. Constant picket duty replaced drill as the order of the day. This duty could be tedious, but it also could be deadly. On May 16, 1864, twenty foragers from the 5th USCT's pickets came into an ambush by approximately sixty Confederate soldiers. Most of the Union soldiers and their lieutenant escaped the trap by fleeing into the woods, but the remainder stayed to return the fire. Of these, nine fell into rebel hands. Five were wounded in the ambush, but two unwounded soldiers escaped their captors after one, a sergeant, shot two rebels with a pistol. The rebels chased the men with hounds, but after the soldiers shot two more men the Confederates gave up the hunt. Two of the wounded soldiers took advantage of the confusion to hide from the Confederates and were rescued by a relief force sent out to help them. Of the remaining five captives, the rebels killed one who was too badly injured to travel, one escaped a day later, and the other three became prisoners of war.[28]

These 5th USCT soldiers who became prisoners of war did not die at the hands of their captors. The three who remained in Confederate hands for more than a day went on to captivity in Salisbury, North Carolina, and Andersonville, Georgia. All three received their paroles in March 1865 and were released to Federal custody at North East Ferry, North Carolina.[29]

The Confederate forces continued to test the resolve of the 5th USCT pickets. Lieutenant Colonel Shurtleff was on hand for an attack by rebel cavalry on May 19, and he noted that although it was his first involvement since their arrival at City Point, the pickets had been engaged in hard and almost constant fighting for more than a

week. The men responded well to the new duty. They had reveille
at three o'clock, and half of the regiment at a time performed picket
duty. The Confederates continued to harass the pickets and captured another 5th USCT soldier. Private Peyton Fry of E Company
joined his comrades in prison at Salisbury. The regiment's leadership felt that the experience had a hardening effect on the soldiers.
Shurtleff commented, "The men of our regiment make the most
excellent soldiers. I never saw better pickets."[30] The regiment would
need the hardening as they joined in the assault on Petersburg.

In the spring of 1864, Ulysses S. Grant was promoted to lieutenant general. Grant intended to take advantage of the Union
army's numerical advantage by keeping constant pressure on the
Confederate forces. He set out to attack General Robert E. Lee's
Army of Northern Virginia with the Union Army of the Potomac.
He also sent General William T. Sherman's army against General
Joe Johnston. General Butler's Army of the James advanced against
lightly defended Petersburg. Grant's plan should have worked. The
overstretched rebels could not defend everywhere. At Petersburg,
the Union achieved a substantial advantage.

The first major battle for the 5th USCT was as part of the XVIII
Corps during the early days of the assault on and siege of Petersburg.
The corps, under the command of General William Smith, had an
opportunity to seize Petersburg. However, the sight of the imposing
breastworks made Smith hesitate. He did not realize that General
P. G. T. Beauregard had far too few troops to man the breastworks
effectively. It was not until near sunset on June 15 that Smith
ordered the corps, including the 5th USCT, to attack.

This assault was the first test of the men's ability to attack entrenched opposition. Their leaders were apprehensive. During their
approach march, the brigade came under fire from a four-gun Confederate battery positioned in a dense copse and supporting infantry
in entrenched positions. The 2nd Brigade commander, Colonel Duncan, ordered his four regiments to attack the Confederate positions.
Duncan arrayed his assault force with three regiments abreast and
one regiment in reserve. The regiments formed two lines, with the
5th USCT at the right of the formation. The charge became confused
as the soldiers traversed the thickly wooded area. The 4th USCT,
in the center of the line, emerged into a clearing before the other
regiments. This clearing was directly in front of the Confederate

guns. Realizing their danger, the 4th USCT gave a yell and charged the cannons. They took 120 casualties in a few minutes as the rebels fired canister into their closely packed ranks. The 5th and the 22nd USCT took advantage of the Confederate concentration to charge the first Confederate line, sweeping into the rebel works. They drove off the gunners and captured two of the cannon.

After reorganizing, the brigade advanced on the next line of Confederate defensive works. These works overlooked Jordan's field, giving the Confederate gunners more than six hundred yards of open ground to their front. Duncan ordered the 5th USCT to advance as skirmishers to try to silence the Confederate guns, but the musket fire from the supporting Confederate infantry prevented the Ohio soldiers from advancing close enough for the Union tactic to be effective. Duncan then repeated his tactic of attacking with three regiments forward. He formed the brigade and conducted a direct assault on the rebel lines. The charge was successful, and the brigade captured five artillery positions and six cannon. Further assaults carried the second rebel line, but General Smith, fearing that General Lee would bring up reinforcements, called off the attack. The following day the brigade returned to Point of Rocks after elements of the VI Corps relieved it.[31]

Smith had missed a real opportunity. Beauregard wrote, "Petersburg at that hour was clearly at the mercy of the Federal commander, who had all but captured it."[32] Confederate troops arrived on June 16 to reinforce Beauregard's positions, and Federal attacks over the next two days failed to make a breakthrough. Generals Smith and Butler were plagued by hesitation and indecision. They would continue to squander opportunities over the course of the Petersburg siege by their unwillingness to press home the attack. For Butler, this trait would finish his career by year's end.

Despite the corps' failure to reach Petersburg, the USCT regiments had performed capably. In his report to the division, 2nd Brigade commander Colonel Duncan lauded his African-American soldiers, saying, "The colonel commanding finds abundant occasion for rejoicing over the important successes of the day and the splendid behavior of the troops. The troops were all untried in battle, and by many it was still a problem whether the Negro would fight. The events of the day justify the most sanguine expectations for the future."[33]

The division commander, General E. W. Hinks, was also pleased, if somewhat more cautious. He wrote, "Colored men, when properly officered and drilled, will not only make soldiers, but the best of soldiers of the line." He then warned, "We should be cautious lest we imperil the success of the project of arming colored men, as well as the success of our armies, by assuming that the negro is a soldier ready made, rather than that he will make a soldier by patient, persistent, and intelligent drill and instruction."[34] In the opinion of their leaders, these African-American soldiers had measured up.

Detractors were quick to denounce the reports, however. The (Columbus) *Crisis,* a Peace Democrat paper, offered a few complaints:

> White soldiers must be fast deteriorating by these reports [of] the assault at Petersburgh [*sic*], under Smith, [USCT soldiers] did the bravest of work, and were especially complimented. This is rather hard on the white soldiers who have done so much and fought so long to wipe out slavery. . . . It is not only not fair, but it is absolutely unjust.[35]

There apparently was nothing the soldiers could do to win the approval of the entrenched racist elements of society. However, their conduct had justified the effort required to get the Ohio African Americans into uniform.

Captain Orlando Brockway sustained a fatal wound in the assault and died the next day. His wife, who was teaching reading to nearby contrabands, was able to be with him when he died. Several of the regiment's officers had their wives near their camps; many, like Mrs. Brockway, involved themselves in philanthropic work.[36]

Even though the regiment had been in several skirmishes, the casualty rate remained surprisingly low and the men were in good health. In April 1864, the regiment still had more than eight hundred soldiers listed on the rolls.[37] The attack on Petersburg claimed only four killed and thirty-one wounded. Following the failed attacks, both armies began to dig in. The rebels continued to improve their breastworks and trenches. To the bulk of the Union force, the Confederate breastworks seemed impregnable. After several abortive efforts to induce their soldiers to attack, Federal commanders relented. Grant concluded, "We will rest the men and use the spade for their protection."[38] The Federal troops constructed an elaborate series of trenches encircling the Confederate lines.

The 5th USCT spent the last week of June and all of July in the trenches in front of Petersburg. Duty in these trenches changed the regiment's casualty rate dramatically. The constant sniping from the Confederate lines wounded and killed soldiers, but the natural conditions were the real killers. The trenches did not have overhead cover, so the soldiers were constantly exposed to the sun or to the rain. This period was one of severe hardship, and the regiment suffered large losses. In C Company, for example, First Sergeant Holland wrote that by July 24, four of the original eighty C Company soldiers had died, two in combat and two from disease.[39] The trimonthly report for July showed that the average strength for the companies dropped from 77 to 58. During this period, 116 soldiers fell sick or wounded; all but 4 of these went into the hospital. Typhoid fever and sunstroke were the primary causes, but some soldiers also injured themselves erecting breastworks and improving the trenches.[40]

All of the regiment's senior leadership fell ill at some time during the summer. Colonel Conine left the regiment with a complaint of illness the week after the regiment's June 15 assault. The regimental surgeon could find nothing wrong with him. Because Conine had applied for a sick leave, he went before a medical board of examination. The board confirmed the surgeon's finding, noting that "his illness was trifling, not entitling him to be absent from his command."[41] Lieutenant Colonel Shurtleff and Major Terry also fell ill for short periods, but neither of these men left the regiment.

By midsummer, the trenches had become an extensive network. The 5th USCT's trench had three lines. The picket trench was closest to the enemy; at some points it was only fifty yards from the rebel picket line. The main trench line, with its rifle pits, lay another hundred yards to the rear of the picket line. It had an embankment to the enemy's side so that the men could walk along the trench without being exposed to enemy sharpshooters. The third trench, where the soldiers rested and ate, was another hundred yards behind the main line of battle. Artillery pits lay among the regiment's position to support their defense.[42]

The trenches, while extensive, were an unpleasant, dangerous place for the 5th USCT. The Army of the Potomac had stalled in front of Petersburg. The weather in the summer of 1864 brought a hot, dusty drought to the men in the trenches. Lieutenant Elliott Grabill described the regiment's experience in the trenches as a period of "rest—a rest in skirmishing, deadly and constant" and "rest under a southern sun, with scanty water and choking dust."[43] In July and August, the regiment performed seemingly endless fatigue details, which had to be done at night because of the danger of Confederate snipers. Even this precaution did not preclude the loss of some of the men to the rebel sharpshooters.

These sharpshooters picked off two 5th USCT officers while the regiment served in the trenches. One was Captain Charles Oren, the commander of Company E. Oren, who was the only commander with no previous military service, had been in charge of a fatigue detail improving a mortar battery position on the night of July 27. The men completed the detail as the sun was rising and prepared for their relief. Oren stepped out of the trench and immediately fell, mortally wounded by a Confederate marksman. The ball struck Oren in the upper thigh and glanced upward into his abdomen. He died later that day. Oren's death provided an opportunity for an insight into the bonds that formed between the regiment's officers and men.

Captain Oren cared for his men. He often discussed them in letters to his wife. This compassion struck a chord among his men, who felt his loss keenly. Sergeant Dillon Chavers wrote to Oren's widow to express his condolences. His words illustrate the bond between Oren and his men. "If my Brother Had of Bin shot it would Not of Hurt me any worse then It Did when He was shot. He Was a good officer not only That But He Had His men At Heart. I Dearly loved him. Any thing that I could Do for Him I would Do it . . . Our Company Has Bin of no use Since His Deth." Chavers, who walked two miles to the medical station to see Oren's body, ended the letter by forgiving a note for thirty-nine dollars that Oren had borrowed from him. He concluded that Oren had been a real friend to his men.[44]

First Lieutenant Edwin Smith died in much the same manner as Captain Oren. He was hit by a rebel sharpshooter while on duty in the trenches on August 12. Smith had been a student at Oberlin College at the opening of the war. Like Lieutenant Colonel Shurtleff and several other of the regiment's officers, he enlisted in Company C, 7th OVI, for one hundred days. After his initial enlistment, Lieutenant Smith reenlisted for three years. Soon thereafter, in a battle at Cross Lanes, Virginia, on August 25, 1861, he became a prisoner of war. Smith was released after a twelve-month imprisonment and worked as a mustering agent until he accepted a commission to serve with the 5th USCT.[45]

Despite the loss of these officers, comparatively few of the enlisted soldiers fell to the rebel gunfire. The tri-monthly Consolidated Morning Report for May through July listed no soldiers killed in action at Petersburg. It seems likely that the Confederates took special care to pick off the officers assigned to the colored regiments.[46]

The 5th USCT remained at Petersburg. In early August General Butler transferred them to the 2nd Brigade. The other two regiments in the brigade were the 36th USCT and the 38th USCT. Lieutenant Colonel Shurtleff described these regiments as "undisciplined regiments of contrabands." Shurtleff believed that General Butler made the change to place a veteran regiment into a weak brigade to strengthen the other regiments, but the change meant that his men lost their eagerly anticipated time out of the trenches.[47]

The continued time in the trenches brought some discredit to the regiment. A 5th USCT soldier deserted the regiment, the first to do so since the unit left Ohio. The man who deserted was not an Ohioan but a contraband who had enlisted into the regiment in June 1864. His desertion raised questions about the wisdom of incorporating the largely uneducated, poorly disciplined contrabands into regiments with the Northern African Americans. It also raised questions about the methods of the recruiters and motivations of the contraband enlistees. The deserter, Private Spencer Brown, had complained that "he was no better treated in the army than he was by his former master."[48]

Several other contraband enlistees deserted from Company H on September 2, making it seem more likely that the soldiers were responding to poor treatment by their commander, Captain Erastus Blood. Captain Blood had a dismal record as an officer in the regiment. He resigned at the end of August rather than face court-martial proceedings. The charges that Lieutenant Colonel Shurtleff filed against Captain Blood included cowardice in the face of the enemy and conduct prejudicial to good order and discipline. Captain Blood had run and hid behind a fence during a skirmish with rebel soldiers. He lost the respect of his fellow officers and the men, but Lieutenant Colonel Shurtleff was unable to act against him because

Blood's Democrat connections protected him until Colonel Conine, also a Democrat, left the regiment for an extended period.[49]

The loss of so many officers over the summer meant that the regiment needed new leadership. Lieutenant Colonel Shurtleff took advantage of Conine's continued absence to press for the appointment of Oberlin men to fill the vacancies. The regiment received three new Oberlin officers, Lieutenants Henry Turner, William Ryder, and James Johnson. Shurtleff's recommendation reflected the direction he was bringing to the regiment. He regarded the men's good morals as important as their service, and declared that all three were "admirably adapted to command Colored troops."[50]

The difference in the leadership between Lieutenant Colonel Shurtleff and Colonel Conine was significant. From the beginning of his association with the regiment, Shurtleff had been an advocate for the African American and believed that his position in the 5th USCT was an opportunity to advance the cause of the black race. His devotion to duty, to his men, and to God is a constant theme throughout his words and deeds. While Conine tolerated insubordinate behavior and even profited from illicit behavior, Shurtleff refused to allow his officers to take advantage of their men or to discredit their service. His denunciation of Captain Spear, the Company K commander, Captain Von Heintze, the Company B commander, Captain Blood, the Company H commander, and Captain Fahrion, the Company C commander, is indicative of Shurtleff's zeal for his mission.[51]

September 1864 brought respite for the now-veteran regiment, which left the Petersburg trenches. On August 28, the regiment pulled back from the line at night and marched ten miles to Deep Bottom, a relatively quiet camp on the north bank of the James River. Although there were still Confederates across the river from the regiment's position, Lieutenant Colonel Shurtleff noted that the regiment was "on good terms with them, no picket firing, no singing of bullets or bursting of shells."[52]

While the regiment enjoyed the relative safety from enemy firing, the fatigue details continued. The XVIII Army Corps, under Major General E. O. C. Ord, labored to strengthen its defensive positions. General Grant planned a grand offensive for the fall, but the plan called for the Union forces to make their defensive line strong enough to hold itself. Once this was accomplished, Grant would likely have enough troops to resume the offensive.[53]

Lieutenant Colonel Shurtleff hoped to fill the regiment with Ohio blacks before the offensive. On August 29 he sent a telegram to Governor John Brough, requesting more men. Brough responded to Shurtleff's request by sending him more than 200 one-year recruits. Brough warned Shurtleff that this would be the only direct reinforcement he would get from Ohio. After these recruits, Ohio was going to have to muster all African Americans recruited in the state as unassigned. The Colored Troops Bureau was to take charge of all recruits and distribute the men where they were most urgently needed.[54]

On the eve of the expected offensive, the regiment had the mixed blessing of new recruits. After a year of operating as an understrength unit, the regiment—boosted by a flood of recruits—grew to 1,102 men. The last report before the unit's rapid growth had given the enlisted strength at 760.[55] Throughout the last two weeks of September the regiment struggled to incorporate and train the green soldiers. The regiment also received new lieutenants and had to replace half of its company commanders.

Added to all of this turmoil was the uncertainty of the 5th USCT's command, because of the extended hospitalization of Colonel Conine. The colonel had injured his groin in the June attack on Petersburg and had never recovered sufficiently to return to the regiment. A medical board finally discharged him for disability while he remained in the hospital in Annapolis, Maryland. Lieutenant Colonel Shurtleff commanded the regiment, but until Conine's discharge he could not be promoted to permanent command. The news of Conine's discharge arrived the day before Lieutenant Colonel Shurtleff took the regiment into combat at the Battle of New Market Heights.

5

The Battle of New Market
Heights and Aftermath

T HE LONG, HOT SUMMER of 1864 wore on the armies locked in constant struggle in front of Petersburg. To the nation, the seeming inactivity of the Union force was galling. General Grant's strategy of applying constant pressure on the Confederates, while militarily sound, was unlikely to produce the spectacular results that would preclude a Peace Democrat victory at the polls. The Union forces had closed in on the Confederate positions, pushing the rebels back from the Rapidan River to the Appomattox River. Grant's relentless pressure forced General Lee to place many of his regiments into static defenses to defend the Confederate capital, its approaches, and its routes of supply. However, the Union army was unable to break through the rebel defenses to seize the capital. Both the Lincoln administration and the army needed a Union victory to bolster Northern confidence in the war effort.

September brought signs of hope for the Union cause. General Sherman captured Atlanta on September 2, ending the stalemate in Georgia. Union forces began to receive reinforcements as the one-year regiments that formed that summer arrived in the northern Virginia theater. Confederate deserters claimed that both Petersburg and Richmond were prepared to collapse under the pressure of the continued siege. As a consequence, Grant made plans to increase the pressure by further constricting the flow of supplies to the Confederate defenders.

Grant's original plan called for a large force to capture Wilmington, North Carolina, the last point of entry for blockade runners supplying Richmond. While this force sealed off that city, the main

Union force would cut the Southside Railroad, the last major rail line supplying Richmond. Grant planned to launch this offensive on October 5, 1864.[1]

The siege was as difficult for Lee. Grant's pressure denied the Confederate general the freedom to choose the conditions for battle, a situation to which he had become accustomed. He had sent Lieutenant General Jubal Early into the Shenandoah Valley, hoping that the threat to Washington would once again draw the Federal forces away from the rebel capital. Although Early's force was able to draw away most of the Union VI Army Corps' regiments, Grant kept the main body of the Army of the Potomac and the Army of the James firmly in place against the Confederate forces.

By mid-September, General Lee felt that his forces were too thin to hold back the growing mass of the Federals. He recalled Major General Joseph Kershaw's infantry division and Lieutenant Colonel Wilfred Cutshaw's artillery battalion, hoping that these forces would enable him to break the siege. Major General Phil Sheridan, however, took advantage of General Early's weakened force to defeat the rebels in two consecutive battles, on September 19 and 22. Sheridan's force then cut the line of the Virginia Central Railroad, denying the Confederates around Richmond access to supplies from the Shenandoah Valley. Lee was forced to reinforce Early to avoid further reverses. He returned the infantry division and the artillery battalion, and sent Brigadier General Thomas Rosser's Laurel Brigade of Virginia Cavalry.[2]

Grant seized the opportunity to strike the weakened Confederates. He believed that by increasing the pressure on the defenders of Petersburg, he could both defeat Lee and prevent him from sending more forces to reinforce Early. Whereas before the victories in the Shenandoah Grant had believed he could seal off Wilmington and perhaps take Petersburg, he now believed that Richmond was within his grasp. A reconnaissance with General Ben Butler convinced him that the rebels were weak east of the James River north of Petersburg. Butler was convinced that his Army of the James would be able to roll up the rebel defenders and press on in a decisive thrust to Richmond. While Grant was not certain that Richmond would fall, he believed that the assault would force Lee to draw forces from the Petersburg defenses. Accordingly, he positioned twenty-five brigades from General George Meade's Army of the

Potomac in position to strike the Confederate supply lines south of Petersburg.

General Grant advanced the timetable for his assault. He knew that given enough time, General Lee would move his forces to make the best use of his positions. Grant was unwilling to give this time to his adversary. He set the new date for the attack: September 29, a week earlier than previously scheduled.

This date created major challenges for the XVIII Army Corps. Only the USCT regiments guarding the Deep Bottom bridgehead and digging the Dutch Gap canal were north of the James River (fig. 1). For the attack to succeed, General Butler had to get the rest of his attacking regiments across the river without depleting the forces manning the encircling works. Butler's Army of the James was scattered along the Petersburg trenches on garrison and fatigue duty. He met his manpower requirements by quietly substituting his newly arrived one-year regiments for the veteran regiments in the works. By the night of September 28, Butler's army was prepared for combat.

The Confederate forces defending Richmond were not expecting a concerted attack by the Federal troops. General Lee was in Petersburg, which had been the object of the Union soldiers throughout the summer. He had stationed his best available regiments in the Petersburg trenches to take part in that city's defense. The forces arrayed along the New Market line were regiments of General John Gregg's Texas Brigade and General Henry "Rock" Benning's Georgia Brigade, bolstered by two Virginia Reserve battalions, sixteen pieces of artillery, and a cavalry brigade. The cavalrymen, under Brigadier General Martin W. Gary, also were responsible for patrolling the eastern and northern approaches to the trench lines.

The Union thrust separated into two wings. The right wing, under Major General David Birney, consisted of the X Corps and the XVIII Corps' 3rd Division. The left wing consisted of the two remaining XVIII Corps divisions. This wing was to move north along the Varina Road, defeat the Confederates at the entrenched camp, and advance to Richmond on the Osborne Turnpike. The right wing had the daunting task of storming the New Market Heights before advancing to Richmond along the New Market Road. The attack seemed destined for victory, as more than 26,000 Union forces were to face fewer than 1,800 Confederates in three brigades.

Before daybreak on September 29, the 5th USCT formed up in General Charles Paine's 3rd Division. Despite its recent reinforcement, the 5th USCT fielded only about 540 soldiers for the attack. Most of the regiment's veterans had been detached to continue their guard and fatigue details at Deep Bottom, and at least 125 of the green soldiers remained in camp also. The Ohio regiment was badly understrength in officers, also. Lieutenant Colonel Shurtleff remained in command, but illness, resignations, and dismissal had whittled down his staff to Major Ira Terry and Lieutenant Elliott Grabill, the adjutant. His line officers were equally scarce. Of the ten companies, only Company C went into the battle with more than one officer.

As the regiment prepared for the assault, Lieutenant Colonel Shurtleff told his men that the interests of the whole black race were at stake in the charge they were about to make:

> If you are brave soldiers, the stigma of diminished pay must be removed. And the greater stigma of denying you full and equal rights of citizenship shall also be swept away and your race forever rescued from the cruel prejudice and oppression which have been upon you from the foundation of the government.

The men responded to the commander's speech with loud cheers, crying for Shurtleff to lead them into battle, for there were no cowards among them.[3]

The 2nd Brigade consisted of the 5th, 36th, and 38th USCT regiments under the command of Colonel Alonzo Draper. Colonel Draper's brigade had the left of the line but would follow Colonel Duncan's USCT brigade into the assault.

The fate of Duncan's brigade shows that Paine made several costly errors in deploying his formations. Chief among these mistakes was feeding the brigades into the battle piecemeal. The rebel defenders of New Market Heights had terrain and their defenses on their side and had earlier defeated two Federal corps. Yet when General Paine deployed his troops, he failed to take advantage of their superior numbers. Duncan's brigade attacked alone, except for skirmishers from the 2nd U.S. Colored Cavalry (USCC) to the right of his brigade. All of the remaining regiments waited in reserve (fig. 1).

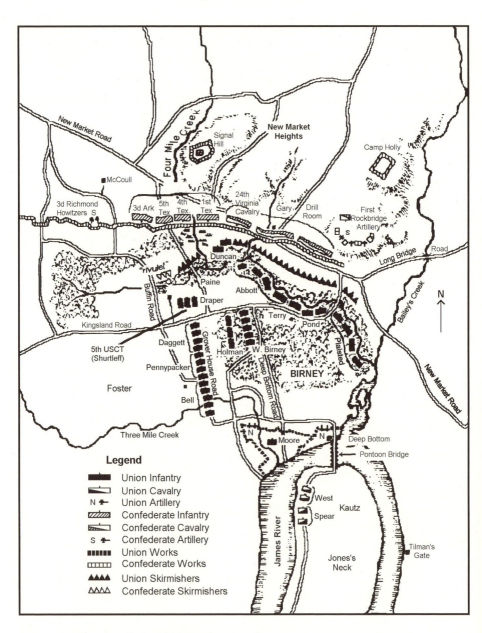

Figure 1. The assault on New Market Heights.

The Confederate position was formidable. Two lines of abatis fronted the parapet. The ground over which the attackers had to cross was swampy and brush covered. Four Mile Creek ran through a shallow ravine parallel to the rebel works. The attackers quickly drove in the Confederate sentinels and skirmishers and advanced on the rebel works. Both the USCT regiments and the rebels held their fire as the African-American soldiers crossed the creek and advanced to the abatis. Once the attackers reached the abatis, the rebels opened fire. The brigade took severe losses, including Colonel Draper, who fell with four wounds. Despite the withering fire, some of the black soldiers made it into the Confederate works, but not enough to take the position. Defenders from other parts of the rebel line, under no pressure, rushed to deal with the invading forces.

The remainder of the brigade retreated under the direction of the 6th USCT's Colonel John Ames. The brigade left scores of wounded on the field, many of whom fell into rebel hands. In less than forty minutes, the brigade lost nearly four hundred casualties. General Paine had not sent in any supporting regiments.

Rather than reconsider the effectiveness of his tactics, Paine chose to repeat the attack. At eight o'clock, he sent Colonel Draper's brigade in unsupported as well. Draper massed his brigade and set off along the same axis as Duncan, straight into the New Market Heights defenses. Unlike Duncan's regiments' abreast formation, Draper's brigade formed into a column by division, presenting only a two-company-wide front to the rebel marksmen.[4]

This time, the Confederates could see the African-American soldiers as soon as they cleared the stream. The 1st Rockbridge Artillery Battery began an intense barrage, and the Texans poured musket fire into the ranks of Union soldiers. The USCT regiments charged toward the Confederate position, but just like Duncan's brigade, they foundered on the abatis. Under the terrible toll of the defenders' fire, the blacks continued to tear down the abatis so that their comrades could push forward. As the regiments' pioneers hacked away at the obstacles, the Confederate marksmen concentrated their fire on the head of the column with telling effect.[5]

Lieutenant Colonel Shurtleff, who had already taken a minie ball through his right hand, fell, shot through the thigh. As he lay wounded, the blood flowing freely from his leg, Shurtleff refused to be carried from the field before seeing his men achieve their objective.[6] Captains Fahrion, Cock, and Ulysses Marvin also became casualties to rebel fire. The attack faltered, much as had the earlier effort, but the 5th USCT's noncommissioned officers took charge of their men, rallying them onward toward the Confederate works. Four of the 5th USCT's first sergeants, Powhatan Beatty, James Bronson, Robert Pinn, and Milton Holland, who was acting sergeant major, took command of Companies D, G, I, and C. These men, who had no chance to rise even to the rank of lieutenant, successfully led their companies in the assault. All four earned the Congressional Medal of Honor for gallantry.[7]

General Butler, who observed the 5th USCT's charge, said,

> It looked in one moment as if it might melt away. The colors of the first battalion went down, but instantly they were up again but with new color bearers. Wonderfully they managed to brush aside the abatis, and then at the double quick the re-formed column charged the second line of abatis. Fortunately they were able to remove that in a few minutes, but it seemed a long time to the lookers on. Then, with a cheer and a yell . . . they dashed upon the fort.[8]

Leading the charge of the 5th USCT into the rebel works fell to Lieutenant Joseph Scroggs's Company H. After Lieutenant Colonel Shurtleff fell wounded, Lieutenant Scroggs's men surged ahead. As they neared the works, Scroggs lost Color Sergeant George Steele, the regimental color bearer, and his orderly sergeant, William Strawder, was wounded in the neck. Orderly Sergeant Strawder, blood streaming from his wound, refused to go to the rear for aid and soon joined his commander in the Confederate position. As the black soldiers clambered over the final embankment, the rebels retreated from their works with little loss.[9]

Again the division's senior leadership squandered the soldiers' effort. Neither General Paine nor General Birney was able to take advantage of the tactical situation. Although only two of the eleven brigades under Birney's command had been engaged, he allowed the Confederates to withdraw to their next line of fortifications rather than attacking them in the open.

Historians have credited the capture of New Market Heights, not to the soldiers' bravery and ability to continue without their leaders, but to General Gregg's belief that the Federal forces advancing along the Varina Road were a greater threat than the loss of New Market Heights.[10] This is an unlikely interpretation, particularly in light of the rebels' subsequent use of the Texas Brigade and the 25th Virginia Battalion. These forces did not rush to fight the Union forces moving up the Varina Road. They moved to positions on the Intermediate Line to await the continued attack from the Union right wing. General Gregg gave the Confederate infantry the order to retreat once it became clear that they would not be able to hold New Market Heights. The 4th USCT's Lieutenant Colonel George Rogers argued that

> the treatment which the rebels have frequently extended to our troops reacts on their cause with beautiful justice. So firmly are they convinced that they will be butchered should they fall into our hands, that they will take no chances as prisoners of ours, and in their solicitude to save themselves they invariably leave their works before we reach them.[11]

Whether the rebels left because the USCT regiments threatened to overrun their position or because the Confederates feared capture, the result was that the soldiers of the 5th USCT, most of whom had only recently arrived from Ohio, followed their leaders into the attack bravely and determinedly.

The 5th USCT planted its colors in the rebel works but soon continued on after the Confederates. The Texans had made it safely to the Exterior Line (fig. 2), and the surviving 5th USCT soldiers joined in the X Corps' assault on those works.

The intent was for the entire 3rd Brigade to push the attack, but the 36th and 38th USCT regiments were not ready to make an assault when General Birney gave the order. The regiment supported Colonel Louis Bell's 3rd Brigade, 2nd Division. Bell's brigade had already received a bloody repulse when the battered remnants of the 5th USCT took the field. Captain Grabill called the order "a most mad enterprise" but noted that the regiment did not hesitate to perform its duty. Despite galling artillery fire, the regiment formed and re-formed its line in preparation for the attack. The three hundred African-American soldiers and their nine remaining officers advanced three-quarters of a mile through slashings of brush, over two ravines, through a crossfire of artillery and small-arms fire, and past where Bell's soldiers were still retreating. As the

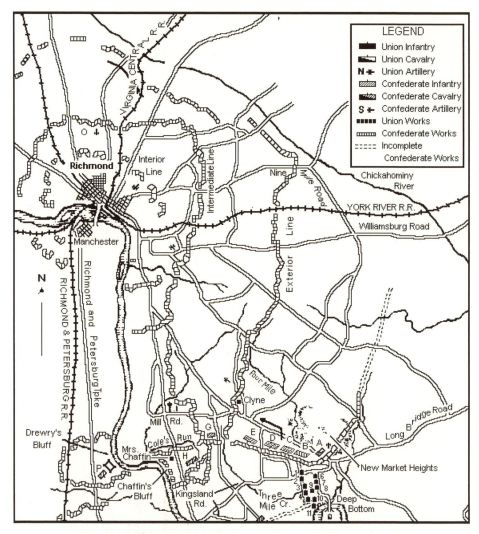

Figure 2. Richmond's defenses, September 1864. Map adapted from Richard J. Sommers, *Richmond Redeemed: The Siege at Petersburg,* 24.

Ohioans broke into the open ahead of the white soldiers, they met a deadly fusillade. Company B's commander, Second Lieutenant Basil Spangler, was wounded in the arm and had to leave the field. Orderly Sergeant Thacker Hall, a nineteen-year-old farmer from Jackson, Ohio, stepped up to take command, but no sooner had he taken charge than a Confederate ball ended his life. Major Terry pressed his men, calling them onward in the hopeless attack. Captain Grabill, who called it the hottest fire he had ever been in, said that the "regiment melted under it, and . . . fell back sullenly—we were too exhausted and too proud to run!"[12]

The regiment, in withdrawing from the field, left their wounded and dead. Twenty-three wounded men, including Company C's Lieutenant John Viers, fell into the rebel's hands. The Confederates, who had an uneven record in their treatment of black troops and their officers, continued in the same vein. They treated the wounded prisoners, including at least three who received amputations, but did not have a high success rate in their treatment.

Of the twenty-three prisoners, eleven died in Confederate hands. Five others met unknown fates after their capture, including Private David Brown, a waiter from Lancaster, Ohio. Brown's prisoner-of-war record shows that he was claimed by R. C. Armisted of Queen Anne's County, Maryland. Brown apparently died in Richmond on November 5, after being enslaved. Seven of the black soldiers and Lieutenant Viers received paroles (see appendix E).[13]

Lieutenant Viers, who had been with the regiment since November 1863, fell captive after being wounded in the leg. He later claimed that he saw the rebels kill wounded black soldiers. Although he knew that his life was still in danger, when the Confederates asked him if he was "not ashamed to command niggers," he replied that he was "proud to be an officer of such an organization."[14] Gallantry was color-blind, and Lieutenant Viers had the courage of his convictions.

Unlike the enlisted soldiers from his regiment, Lieutenant Viers, who was the only officer of the 5th USCT to become a prisoner of war, did not remain long in Confederate confinement. He attributed his release to a mistake on the part of the rebels. The exchange of prisoners had initially been suspended because of Confederate refusals to exchange African-American prisoners and their officers for rebels held by Federal authorities. General Butler, who became commissioner of exchange for the Union during the summer and fall of 1864, decreed that despite the abysmal conditions and suffering of the Union prisoners, no exchanges would be possible until the rebels agreed to treat all Union soldiers captured as prisoners of war. Lieutenant Viers was among the six hundred Union prisoners released on October 9. He was one of two USCT officers freed that day, but another USCT lieutenant had left the prison hospital the previous day. Viers believed that his release was in response to the same order that had freed the other officer.[15]

Despite the apparent break in the prisoner controversy, the Confederates soon reverted to their policy of treating the captured USCTs as property. In a letter to Confederate Captain W. H. Hatch, Major M. P. Turner, commander of the Confederate States Military Prison (Libby Prison) in Richmond, advised the assistant commissioner of exchange that Lieutenant General Richard Ewell ordered him to deliver those African-American prisoners who were able to work for fatigue duty on the rebel fortifications. Major Turner sent 82 black soldiers from the 5th, 7th, and 30th USCT Regiments on October 6 to join 68 other men who had been captured at the Battle of the Crater on July 30.[16] At the same time, Richmond newspapers carried advertisements calling for slaveholders to come to Richmond and claim "certain colored men." General Butler responded to these two acts by ordering 110 Confederate prisoners to perform hard labor digging the Dutch Gap canal until the African-American soldiers were returned to ordinary prisoner-of-war status. General Butler's order specified that the rebels would receive precisely the same treatment as the blacks laboring for the Confederates: the same rations, the same ten-hour daily work detail, and the same threat of instant death for attempted escape. Faced with the concrete proof of "Beast" Butler's resolve, General Lee countermanded General Ewell's order, and the African-American soldiers returned to Libby Prison on October 19.[17]

In their assaults on New Market Heights and Fort Gilmer, the soldiers of the 5th USCT had to overcome not only the stubborn defense of the Confederates but also the poor tactical abilities of their commanding general. Their attempts were not without price. Besides Lieutenant Colonel Shurtleff, 4 company commanders, 2 lieutenants, and 229 other soldiers from the regiment became casualties, including 28 killed and 23 captured or missing.[18]

The soldiers returned to New Market Heights, where they repulsed a rebel counterattack the following day. Of the September 29 action at New Market Heights, General Butler commented, "A few more such gallant charges and to command colored troops will be the post of honor in the American armies. The colored soldiers by coolness, steadiness, and determined courage and dash, have silenced every cavil of doubters of their soldierly capacity."[19]

General Butler specifically noted the gallantry of the 5th USCT's sergeants and declared that he would commission a medal in their honor. He promoted Lieutenant Colonel Shurtleff to colonel for "distinguished gallantry on the field of battle." General Butler further authorized the addition of the inscriptions "Petersburg" and "New Market Heights" to the 5th USCT's regimental colors.[20]

The 5th USCT remained in the trenches it captured at New Market Heights until early December. Like the other regiments in the 3rd Brigade, the 5th USCT had been mauled storming New Market Heights and in the abortive attack on Fort Gilmer. For the 5th, the losses cut through the entire regiment from Colonel Shurtleff down. The regiment was fortunate that replacement officers were already slated to fill vacancies in the regiment and that the regiment was filled beyond its strength immediately before the battles. Despite the losses on September 29 and 30, the regiment reported a strength of 970 at the end of October.[21]

October provided a respite for the Ohio regiment. The 5th USCT found itself on the left end of the Union line between Fort Harrison and the James River. The river ensured that they would not be taken from that side by surprise, and their strong fortifications apparently dissuaded the rebels from attacking their position. The cavalry units to their right fought a heated skirmish with the Confederates on October 7 but drove the rebels back without serious difficulty.[22]

The arrival of the paymaster on October 6 added to the general sense of well-being. The regiment had not received its pay since early in the summer, so the men were "rejoicing over the recent acquisition of a plentiful supply of greenbacks and without much discretion or regard for expenses, going for the contents of the sutler shop." The sutler, Henry Elias, had been warned previously about taking advantage of the men, but apparently the temptation was too great for him. Colonel Draper's policy required the brigade's sutlers to set their prices no higher than fifty cents over cost for their goods. On October 20, Colonel Draper, the brigade commander, ordered Elias and the sutlers for the 36th and 38th USCTs out of the department. While temporarily depriving the men of the comforts that the sutlers provided, Colonel Draper's action showed his care for the men. Draper, like many of the 5th USCT's officers, inspired the men by proving that they fought in a common cause.[23]

Officer assignments for the 5th USCT caused great concern in the officer ranks. Much as he had done in August by shifting the USCT regiments in the XVIII Corps, General Butler upset the relationships among the officers by promoting officers to fill vacancies without reference to their regimental or brigade commanders. Colonel Shurtleff returned to his regiment on October 26 to discover that rather than promoting Major Ira Terry to fill the lieutenant colonel position, General Butler had appointed John B. Cook, late major of the 22nd USCT. General Butler was again inflexible in his decision. He did agree to promote Major Terry to lieutenant colonel—in the 22nd USCT. General Butler then infuriated the 5th USCT's captains by selecting William R. Brazie, late captain of the 22nd USCT, to become the 5th USCT's new major. Despite Colonel Shurtleff's protests, the general would not be persuaded to change his decisions.[24]

Captain Grabill became the Company H commander. He was well pleased with his new command because of the efforts of Orderly Sergeant Strawder. The orderly sergeant had entered the regiment at age eighteen from Lancaster, Ohio, where he had been a barber. Despite his youth and his small (5'4") stature, Strawder kept the men in line. Captain Grabill noted that the men followed Orderly Sergeant Strawder "to the letter." His discussion of Strawder in his correspondence indicates that the men formed a fast bond of respect and trust.

Because of men like Orderly Sergeant Strawder, Colonel Shurtleff, and Orderly Sergeants Pinn, Bronson, Beatty, and Holland, the 5th USCT became a celebrated regiment. Thomas Chester, writing dispatches for the *Philadelphia Press,* noted that the regiment had had the post of honor and danger and had acquitted itself grandly. Colonel Shurtleff wrote that the "5th has gained very great credit by its splendid fighting on the 29th ult. It has the best reputation of any colored regiment in the army."[25]

Indeed, all of the regiments involved in the battles on September 29–30 showed that blacks would fight and could fight. In fact, the 5th USCT's situation showed that the African-American soldier could fight without white officers. Although the regiment never had any blacks commissioned, the leadership abilities of the regiment's noncommissioned officers indicated that there were those who could have easily filled such positions.

Colonel Shurtleff returned to the regiment but continued to use crutches. Because of his injury, he did not accompany the regiment when it marched to Seven Pines on October 27. The movement was an attempt to turn the Confederate line. General Alfred Terry, with the X Corps, was to fix the rebels in the Exterior Line. In the event that he was able to do this, General Godfrey Weitzel's XVIII Corps would sweep around the northern end of the rebel position near the Williamsburg Road. General Butler developed this plan after Confederate deserters informed him that the northern end of the Exterior Line was not manned.[26]

The 5th USCT moved out with the rest of the corps, traveling east, south of the paralleling movement by the X Corps. The regiment reached Seven Pines by two o'clock but found that despite the deserters' reports there were rebels in the works. General Weitzel believed that the forces in the works were nothing more than a brigade of dismounted cavalry, so he ordered in Colonel Joseph Kiddoo's 1st Brigade, 3rd Division. Colonel Kiddoo's brigade, consisting of the 1st, 22nd, and 37th USCT Regiments, met with a bloody repulse, probably because the regiments had a large body of untrained recruits, many of whom broke and ran under the Confederate fire. The 5th USCT, which was in the 2nd Brigade, did not assault the Confederate works because General Weitzel was waiting for orders from General Butler. The regiment spent the afternoon exchanging fire with the rebel pickets. During these exchanges, Lieutenant William Ryder, a new lieutenant, was hit in the hip by a twenty-pound Parrott shell. He was one of seven men in the regiment to be wounded in the action. By the time the orders from corps headquarters arrived, daylight was fading and the XVIII Corps returned to its previous positions without further incident.[27]

November brought the national elections. By Ohio law, those African Americans who were over twenty-one and whose ancestry contained more white than black blood were able to vote. The 5th USCT submitted 194 ballots. Of these, no more than 25 would have represented the officers present for duty. But whether officer or enlisted, the regiment voted 194 to 0 for Lincoln. The Ohioans were the only blacks in the XVIII Corps with even a marginal level of enfranchisement. The regiment was also the only regiment whose ballots contained no votes for McClellan. The regiment's place of polling was a site of much interest for McClellan supporters, but the armed sentries protecting the voters ensured that only the Ohioans cast their ballots there. Orderly Sergeant Strawder was among those who cast his vote for President Lincoln. When the dark-complexioned sergeant was challenged as to his right to vote under the Ohio Constitution, he pointed to the still livid scar on his throat, declaring that "that had earned him a right to vote anywhere." Strawder and the rest of the regiment were gratified to discover that the nation shared their faith in "Father Abraham."[28]

Further gratification for the soldiers came with Thanksgiving. Private subscriptions back home raised money to provide the soldiers with a sumptuous dinner. The Army of the James ensured that its African-American soldiers shared in the bounty, much as they shared in the risks. The men enjoyed turkey, duck, chicken, vegetables, and fruits after a regimental meeting. The men listened to prayers from James Patton, the regiment's recently appointed chaplain, and speeches from the few officers who were on duty with the regiment, and gave three cheers for Abraham Lincoln.[29]

While the Ohioans concentrated on drilling their recruits, integrating their officers, and healing their sick and wounded, the Union leadership was reconsidering the problem of blockade running up the Cape Fear River to Wilmington, North Carolina. Wilmington was the last major port available to the Confederates, and it was defended by the most impressive coastal fortification in the Confederacy—Fort Fisher. General Butler's African-American troops, soldiers whose martial skills were once in question, would form part of the task force that would set out to capture Fort Fisher and the port of Wilmington.

The autumn of 1864 would be the watershed for the 5th USCT. The regiment provided another example for those who claimed that black soldiers were the same as their white counterparts. While there would always be those who would scoff at the idea that the races could ever be equal, at New Market Heights the valor of the officers and men of the 5th USCT showed that these men were as good as any soldiers in the Union. No longer could blacks rationally be considered fit only for fatigue duty. While commanders and soldiers could refuse to use African-American soldiers, they could not honestly say it was because they did not believe that the blacks would fight.

6

Operations in North Carolina, 1864–1865

THE EXPEDITIONS TO FORT Fisher (December 7–27, 1864, and January 3–17, 1865) marked the end of the 5th USCT's service in Virginia. The regiment would return briefly between the two expeditions, but following the capture of the fort, it would campaign in North Carolina for the rest of the war. The move to North Carolina continued the regiment's active involvement in combat operations.

The Army of the James reorganized in December. The principal effect of the War Department's General Order 297 was to increase the level of segregation between the white infantry regiments and the USCT regiments. The order placed all the white infantry regiments previously assigned to the X and XVIII Corps into a new corps, designated the XXIV Corps, under the command of Major General Ord. The USCT regiments from the two corps were now to comprise the XXV Corps under the command of Major General Godfrey Weitzel.[1] The army wasted little time getting its two newest corps into action.

On December 6, General Weitzel received orders to take command of an expeditionary force that was to close the port of Wilmington to rebel blockade runners. The crux of the mission was the capture of Fort Fisher, the Confederate bastion at the mouth of North Carolina's Cape Fear River. Fort Fisher was a vital installation for the Confederates because its guns prevented Union warships from effectively blockading the mouth of the river. Rebel blockade runners used this river to bring supplies into the port of Wilmington. If the Union forces took Fort Fisher, the rebels would lose an important avenue of supply for their Army of Northern Virginia.

The blockade of Wilmington was not successful. Despite the efforts of more than thirty Union warships intercepting the blockade runners, more than 3 million dollars of supplies and munitions entered the port in 1864. The Union navy had captured or destroyed sixty ships, but the extreme profits for the blockade runners ensured that they would continue to test the Federal presence.

Unlike the other Confederate ports that had succumbed to the Union blockade, Wilmington had three factors that had kept it viable throughout the war. The first was the peculiar geography of the mouth of the Cape Fear River, which opened onto Smith's Island and the Frying Pan Shoals. This provided two entrances to the river, separated by more than twenty miles of dangerous shallows. The Federal blockade had to patrol an arc of more than fifty miles to close off the mouth of the river, which it never successfully did. The second factor was Wilmington's location, nearly twenty miles from the river's mouth, well beyond the range of Federal warships. Neither of these factors alone would have prevented the Union from sealing off the port; but coupled with the presence of Fort Fisher, they kept Wilmington open long into the war.[2] Any hope of closing Wilmington would first require the capture of Fort Fisher.

Closing the formidable fortress complex had been on the mind of General Grant through the fall. He believed that the closure of the port would hasten the collapse of General Lee's Army of Northern Virginia. Much like his decision to attack the Confederate defenses between Petersburg and Richmond, his decision to assault Fort Fisher came as the result of events in other theaters. General Sherman's march through Georgia had led rebel leaders to send many of the North Carolina defenders south to help deal with the freewheeling Union general. Grant saw the depleted garrison as an invitation to attack.[3]

The plan for the assault on Fort Fisher was audacious, complicated, and fraught with opportunities for General Butler to fail. The operation required coordination between General Butler and Admiral David Porter, who commanded the naval squadron assigned to the expedition. Grant intended for General Weitzel to command the army troops, but Butler, perhaps seeing the enormous potential for glory in capturing the South's greatest bastion, took advantage of his position as Weitzel's direct superior to assume the command. This spelled disaster for the expedition, because Porter and Butler despised each other. Butler had openly criticized Porter's role in the capture of New Orleans in 1862, and the two men had been unable to exchange civil words since that time.[4]

Because of this lack of coordination between the two flag officers, the expedition never achieved its goals. The expedition certainly had the assets it needed to accomplish the task. Butler's troops for this expedition consisted of infantry regiments from both corps of the Army of the James. The 6,500-man Union force left Virginia in a navy flotilla on December 14. After some deceptive sailing, the infantry regiments arrived on December 16. However, the supporting naval squadron of fifty-six warships did not arrive until December 18, when the weather became unfavorable for landing troops. The storm continued, so Butler sent his transports to Beaufort, North Carolina, to take on coal and water.

On board the ocean steamer *John Rice,* the 5th USCT was crowded and uncomfortable. The steamer carried the regiment's 900 soldiers, the horses of the staff, and the regiment's draft animals. The soldiers had little opportunity to go onto the deck to take fresh air, except for their shifts on deck watch. Lieutenant Scroggs, writing in his diary while the fleet lay waiting for its naval escorts, commented on the beautiful weather and pleasant conditions. He recognized their location by the imposing sight of Fort Fisher. He commented acerbicly, "Either we are not to land here or the expedition is commanded by a lunatic." The good weather would only continue until December 18. By then, the men had spent nine days aboard the ship in high seas and mystery. Although the opportunity for betraying the mission was past, Butler still had not informed his regimental commanders of their objective. Colonel Shurtleff called their movements "entirely deceptive." He guessed that they were to attack Wilmington but felt that if that were the case, they had missed their chance with the passing of the clear weather.[5]

Admiral Porter made the unilateral decision to blow the powder boat just after midnight on Christmas Eve. This decision infuriated General Butler; but as it turned out, the powder boat detonation had no effect on the fort. After a lengthy naval bombardment, 2,500 Union infantry landed, including the Ohioans of the 5th USCT. Lieutenant Scroggs and Company H came ashore under fire from Confederate skirmishers, but the rebels beat a hasty retreat when the size of the Union force became evident. The regiment took no casualties but spent much of the afternoon waiting to oppose Confederate reinforcements that might attempt a relief of the fort's garrison while Butler decided whether to attempt an assault. He decided not to try, despite indications—as clear as the surrender of groups of Confederate defenders and the capture of the fort's flag by a lieutenant in General Adelbert Ames's division—that the fort was his for the taking.[6] The troops returned to their transports, and the naval warships resumed their bombardment of the fort. The weather turned foul again, causing General Butler to order his force back to Virginia.[7]

Officers in the 5th USCT expressed their disbelief at their withdrawal. Colonel Shurtleff "felt sure of the capture of Fort Fisher" once the soldiers made a successful landing and deemed General Butler's orders a "profound mystery." Chaplain Patton noted that the men were ashamed to know that they had failed without even trying. The men, Patton said, wanted to immediately put back out to sea to attack Fort Fisher.[8]

Although Confederate gunfire wounded only two soldiers, General Butler's nerve failed, much as it had done at Petersburg in June. His desire to have everything his way kept him from pushing his soldiers to gain the prize. Butler's inability to read the enemy defenses and his unwillingness to accept the counsel of his subordinates ensured his failure. This time, his failure was too much for General Grant. He pushed President Lincoln to remove Butler from command. Even Butler's political connections were no longer strong enough to protect him from the consequences of his hesitation. Lincoln relieved Butler of his command on January 4, 1865.

General Butler had been a friend and an advocate of the African-American soldier throughout the war. He had ensured that the soldiers under his command were treated as fairly as possible. He was, however, not a good commander. He failed on several opportunities to take advantage of chances for victory that his troops had won. Colonel Shurtleff saw Butler's dismissal with mixed emotions. He believed that the general had always had the USCT regiments' best interests at heart, yet Shurtleff acknowledged that he "believe[d] the interests of the country are best served by his removal. He was wholly unfit to command an army in the field. I have no doubt his great ability will be made use of elsewhere where it will be effective for good."[9]

Union leadership still wanted to take Fort Fisher. Porter had not removed his squadron when Butler returned the troops to Virginia, so Grant moved rapidly to return the soldiers to Fort Fisher—under a new commander. Major General Alfred Terry commanded the force returning to take Fort Fisher. Terry and Porter had few difficulties coordinating their plans. Porter's bombardment was effective not only in pinning down the defenders but also in disabling many of the fort's guns.

The 5th and other USCT regiments in General Paine's division returned to the Fort Fisher expedition over the protests of Admiral Porter. He told Assistant Secretary of the Navy Gustavus Fox, "We want white men here—not niggers."[10] Unlike the Army of the James leadership, Porter still viewed the black soldiers with suspicion and hostility. Grant, however, did not change his troops, and the African-American soldiers once again steamed south.

On this journey, the 5th USCT drew more comfortable berths. They shared the steamship *Champion,* a 1,600-passenger ocean liner from the California Line, with the 1st USCT and General Paine's staff. Once at sea, however, the flotilla ran into rough weather. The night of January 7, *Champion* broke her steering mechanism and began to founder. Lieutenant Scroggs, nervously clutching at "cork fixins," thought that the ship would roll over, but the crew repaired the damage and they soon rejoined the convoy. The storm continued through January 10, and the ships were forced to put in to Beaufort harbor. The morning of January 11 dawned clear, and the flotilla put back out to sea.[11]

General Terry split the army troops into two elements: the four XXIV Corps brigades formed the assault force; the 5th USCT, along with the other eight USCT regiments of the XXV Corps' 3rd Division, formed the defensive force. The 5th USCT, under the command of Major Brazie, landed three miles north of the fort and immediately began to fortify its position against the expected relief column. The USCT regiments successfully prevented rebel relief forces from aiding Fort Fisher's defenders. In his report on the loss of Fort Fisher, Confederate General Braxton Bragg noted that the USCT regiments had thrown up fifteen- to twenty-foot-high breastworks all along their 450 yards of front and had erected a line of sharpened palisades to deter rebel assaults. He declined to attack, recognizing that he would be wasting soldiers in a hopeless endeavor.[12] The XXIV Corps troops, with the reinforcement of the 27th USCT, carried the fort, but not without taking serious casualties. The 5th USCT, because its role did not call for it to assault the fort, did not suffer loss during the operation. Without Fort Fisher's protection, the blockade running ended.

Although circumstances dictated that the USCT regiments did not have a fighting role in the capture of Fort Fisher, they expected to have to defend against a reinforcing column. The experience they had gained in the Petersburg trenches made them adept at fortifying their position. It was the imposing field fortifications that prevented the relief column from attempting to attack the Federal forces. Without the veteran USCT soldiers, the assault could have ended much differently.

The 3rd Division stayed at Fort Fisher after the assault. The soldiers had left their baggage in Virginia, so they spent the next three weeks without a change of clothing or bedding. The soldiers were eager to continue the campaign, believing that it would be the last of the war. Colonel Shurtleff believed that the move to North Carolina meant the regiment would take part in operations that would have more visible results.

General John Schofield's XXIII Corps arrived from Tennessee to reinforce the Union soldiers the first week of February. On February 11, the Federal force took part in the march on Wilmington, twenty miles from Fort Fisher. General Paine deployed the 5th USCT as his skirmishers, and they quickly covered the first several miles. Ten miles from the city, the Union soldiers encountered General Bragg's Confederates in entrenched positions at Sugar Loaf. The Federal soldiers marched close to the rebel lines, drove in their pickets, and entrenched their own positions.

The 5th USCT settled into the trenches with an ease that demonstrated their veteran status. The men quickly located wood, constructed bomb proofs, and shored up the walls of their trenches. Captain Grabill noted that "it seemed more natural to be close under the works of the enemy and face to face with our mortal foes." In contrast to their experience at Petersburg, the Ohioans found that General Robert Hoke's North Carolina brigades had no interest in constant sniping. One of Captain Grabill's men remarked, "We have met these fellows so often that fighting is no novelty and killing no pastime."[13]

For the next seven days, as the USCT soldiers pinned down General Hoke's troops, the soldiers from the XXIII Corps tried to flank the Confederate forces by crossing the Cape Fear River and attacking Fort Anderson on the western bank. General Jacob Cox led the Union advance, which included the support of Admiral Porter's monitors and gunboats. The Confederates held out briefly, but on February 19, the rebels on both sides of the river abandoned their lines. The bluecoats moved into the Confederate positions on Sugar Loaf and Fort Anderson, and the Union leadership considered its next move.

General Paine again deployed the 5th USCT as skirmishers. This time, the Confederates contested the Union advance, and the column made slow progress. However, the rebels could only slow the advance, as the powerful Union force marched cautiously up the peninsula, pushing the Confederates from each attempted position. Captain Grabill noted that "the Southern chivalry speak with contempt of the 'smoked Yankees,' yet they fell back with due respect before a well conducted skirmish line of 'colored Americans of African descent.'" The Union soldiers pursued the fleeing rebels, but the Confederates made it into a second line five miles from Wilmington.[14]

This line of defenses was strong. The remainder of Hoke's brigade occupied it with the support of several pieces of artillery. As an added measure, Wilmington's defenders had dammed a stream so that the approaches to the works flooded. The 5th USCT led the charge, often in water up to the men's waists. The regiment advanced to within fifty yards of the Confederate guns, but the galling rebel fire took its toll on the black soldiers, wounding thirty-nine of them. Surprisingly, not one of the Ohioans was killed in the assault.[15]

The attackers again entrenched before the Confederate position, but General Bragg had had enough. The night of February 21 the rebels again evacuated their positions. The Union troops marched into Wilmington on February 22 with only token opposition.[16]

General Paine pushed the division through Wilmington in hopes of capturing General Bragg's force intact. The Union soldiers caught up with the Confederate rear guard at their pontoon bridge over the North East River. The Federals captured the pontoon bridge, but the main body of the rebels escaped.

The 5th USCT returned to Wilmington, where the steamer *Daniel Webster* arrived with the regiment's camp equipment, documents, personal effects, and those soldiers who had not been well enough to travel with the attackers of Fort Fisher. The soldiers' delight at the thought of having a change of clothing for the first time in over a month quickly evaporated. As the horrified soldiers watched, the *Daniel Webster* sank at dockside, carrying their belongings down with it. Over the next two weeks, the soldiers waited for salvage crews to bring up those items that could be rescued. Most would wait in vain.[17]

For the soldiers of the 5th USCT, the ordeals of combat were finished. The war continued, however, and the soldiers, now a part of the X Corps under General Sherman, would finish the war as many in the North had envisioned the role of the African-American soldier. They marched in the rear of General Sherman's columns, guarding his trains as the Federal troops traversed the state to pin down General Joe Johnston and the last rebel forces.

For the Ohio soldiers, the foraging that was prevalent in the fast-moving columns of General Sherman's corps was disturbing. The 5th USCT had become accustomed to either having the army provide their supplies or going without, but they were an anomaly among their new comrades. Colonel Shurtleff found the foraging little better than pillaging and plundering. He termed the activities of the soldiers disgraceful and refused to allow his troops to participate. Shurtleff called for a system of foraging that did not denude the civilians in the path of war of all they possessed. When his soldiers needed food on the march, he had them range away from the column and instructed them to take only what the households could spare. Shurtleff recognized that many of the Southerners might have deserved such harsh treatment for their rebellion, but he felt that the loss of discipline and the misery that the rampant foraging created would unnecessarily harm both the soldiers and their victims.[18]

During the weeks of marching, the regiment realized that the Confederacy was finished. Gone forever was the fear that the "Peace Commissions" that had flourished in January would steal the significance of the war from the black race. Colonel Shurtleff wrote that he thanked God that the nation's military and civilian leaders were such that they would not make a settlement with the rebels on the basis of protecting slavery. If for nothing else, their service had helped to achieve that worthy end.[19]

The regiment did not fight again, but the men were cheered to learn that the Confederacy was no more. In late April, the regiment participated in a review in Raleigh honoring General Sherman. Following the review, the regiment moved to a site in the woods outside the city. It seemed clear that the army would be remaining in the South for several months after the end of the war.[20]

The regiment, their days as a combat unit over, settled into camp life with a will. They only remained near Raleigh for few days before marching to Goldsboro on April 29. There the regiment began to guard the railroad lines and bridges against disaffected rebels. Again the regiment set up camp outside the city. Colonel Shurtleff began to arrange to have the soldiers take classes to improve the literacy in the regiment. His goal was to "have every soldier be able to write his name and read a letter in the New Testament."[21]

The regiment built a significant camp at Goldsboro. Like the camp at Raleigh, this one was situated in a wooded area. The regiment took pains to lay out the camp so that it was both functional and aesthetic. Each company had its own street in the camp; each street was wide enough to muster the company and to march the platoons to regimental drill. The soldiers had eighteen wood-sided houses per company. They constructed arbors covered with pine boughs to shade their houses and had kept trees to act as screens around the camp. Each company street had an arch with that company's letter at its crest.[22]

Life in the camp was simple; but for many, the desire to return home was powerful. Unlike the men, who had to serve out the term of their enlistment, the officers could submit their resignations. Colonel Shurtleff, Quartermaster Marsh, Chaplain Patton, Captain Fahrion, and Lieutenants Lucian Chapin and Jacob Skinner all submitted their resignations. The men, who had no such method of returning home, tried to make their camp as much like home as possible. The regimental band, the "Ebony Tooters," continued to play in the evenings for the entertainment of the regiment.[23]

The Ebony Tooters was a volunteer band that the men of the regiment formed in December 1864, although the idea for the group had come as early as the previous summer. The soldiers bought their instruments for six hundred dollars, which they raised themselves, and apparently taught themselves to play over the months. In January, Lieutenant Scroggs commented that they had "made rapid progress and can already (only one month) discourse enchanting music, especially when not attempting to play any particular tune." In February, Shurtleff, who apparently had more demanding tastes in music, noted that while his soldiers had musical talent, they needed a teacher very much. By May, despite their inability to find a teacher, Shurtleff regarded them as much improved.[24]

The 5th USCT's role in the standing army was that of local police. They found that the task was difficult not only because of their race but also because the depredations of Sherman's soldiers had turned the very uniform they wore into a symbol of fear. Despite this, the regiment sent out detachments to the area around Goldsboro to be provost marshals and to help restore order to the countryside. They found themselves becoming involved in settling disputes between neighbors, protecting the freedmen from their former masters, and in some cases preventing the freedmen from mistaking freedom for unlimited license.[25]

By all accounts, the soldiers and officers had a fairly easy life in Goldsboro. The risks of war, the stresses of life in the trenches, the constant exposure to both enemy fire and the elements, were all past. However, for Colonel Shurtleff, the easy life, while lucrative, was not why he had answered the call to arms. He felt that his role in helping to "thoroughly dispel the cruel hatred of the black race" was complete.[26]

Before he left for home, Colonel Shurtleff gave a farewell address to the soldiers of the 5th USCT.

> The relation which has so long existed between you and myself is severed. For nearly two years your interests have been my interests. Together we have had our part in hard marches, trying sieges, and bloody battles. Together we have wept over fallen comrades—together rejoiced in successes achieved and victories won. Your record is one of which you may well be proud. God will reward you for your sacrifices and a grateful country appreciates your services. Thanking you for your uniform kindness and prompt obedience, I bid you an affectionate farewell.[27]

Colonel Shurtleff's departure brought Lieutenant Colonel John Cook into command of the regiment. The twenty-six-year-old officer from Lewiston, Maine, had been a major in the 22nd USCT until General Butler's spate of promotions following the Battle of New Market Heights. Cook had been wounded at Sugar Loaf outside Wilmington and had been erroneously discharged when his treatment took him outside the theater. However, his absence did not stop the energetic officer from making his mark on the last, troubled months of the regiment's existence.[28]

The 5th USCT moved from its pleasant arbor outside Goldsboro to a swampy site outside New Berne. The mission of the regiment changed from a decentralized local police force to a garrison for the fortifications around the city. New Berne hosted a large population of freedmen who had come to New Berne in 1862 when General Ambrose E. Burnside captured the city and had stayed under the protection of the Union troops for the remainder of the war. The excitement and gaiety of the "free town" would prove too much for many of the regiment's men. Soldiers wandered away from the camp, returning only for roll call. By July, Lieutenant Colonel Cook felt compelled to forbid his soldiers to possess civilian clothing. Without civilian clothing, the soldiers found it much more difficult to blend in with civilians once they left camp. In August, the regiment resorted to holding roll calls five times a day to prevent the soldiers from wandering away. Despite these measures, some of the men still had to face individual punishment to curb their indiscipline. Of the eighteen disciplinary actions taken by the commander between June and September, eleven were for leaving the camp without permission.[29]

The summer months in North Carolina exposed the regiment to the deleterious effects of extended camp life. While the regiment soon built wooden barracks, there was no escaping the pervasive humidity and heat. Despite rigorous efforts by the leaders to keep the soldiers clean and healthy, the regiment's morale and strength dwindled.

Although the camp was neat and orderly, the men and officers fell ill to malaria and related maladies. Cook came down with intermittent fever severe enough to send him to the hospital for a week at the end of July. Several of the other officers also fell ill, including Lieutenants Turner and Albert Safford, whose cases of chronic diarrhea incapacitated them. Both of these officers returned to Oberlin, where they remained until the unit mustered out in September.

After the Battle of New Market Heights the regiment still num-
bered 970 men and officers. The only battle losses after that were
the 39 wounded at Wilmington. Three hundred men left the regiment in August because they had only enlisted for one year. Yet
by September, the number of effectives had dropped to 489.[30] In
Company C, for example, after the Battle of New Market Heights,
only 2 soldiers would be wounded by Confederate bullets, but 18
would contract one of the many "camp" diseases. Of these 18, 7
died in Union hospitals or in camp.[31] The disease mortality rate
of 21 percent among the original members of the 5th USCT is 50
percent higher than the 1-in-7 rate for all African-American soldiers,
and more than triple the 1-in-17 rate for white Union soldiers.[32] As a
regiment, the 5th USCT had the eighth-highest casualty rate among
the 163 regiments of the USCT.[33]

The 5th USCT's service came to an abrupt end. The African-
American soldiers were a source of constant irritation to the still-
proud South. As a means of helping to speed Reconstruction,
President Andrew Johnson ordered all the USCT regiments recruited in the North mustered out immediately. The Ohio regiment
received its muster-out order on September 10, 1865. The unit
promptly began to get its rolls, accounts, and equipment ready.
Ten days later, a train bearing the regiment pulled into the depot
at Columbus, Ohio. The soldiers received little attention on their
return. The war had been over for nearly half a year, and the country
had returned to civilian pursuits. The men filed up to the paymaster
to settle their accounts with the army. They received their back pay
and a bounty of one hundred dollars. These soldiers, who had left
Ohio nearly two years previously, would soon return to a life not
much different in the main from that which they had left. Many
would not live to see the changes that their service had accelerated,
but they knew that when their race, and what is more important,
their country, had called, they had answered.

7

Conclusion

DURING THEIR TWO YEARS of service, the 5th USCT saw significant changes in the status of blacks and of African-American soldiers—changes that often resulted from the example the soldiers set. Their courage on the battlefield, their fortitude on the march, and their willingness to perform whatever role their leaders required of them helped to demonstrate that these were men. Union leadership responded to the evident humanity of its black soldiers by making changes in their status that narrowed the gulf between the African-American and white soldiers.

The most concrete of these changes came in the area of the African-American soldier's pay. The War Department, which initially paid the black soldier far less than his white counterpart, equalized pay for all soldiers by the war's end. The army also paid the soldiers the bounty that the Union had previously said blacks were not authorized to receive. The soldiers saw this pay as a sign that the army, at least, believed in their equality before the law.

Another symbol of the government's acceptance of the black soldier was the steadfast refusal of the Lincoln administration to accept the parole of prisoners until the Confederates agreed to treat African-American soldiers the same as white soldiers. This policy could not prevent individual rebels from mistreating black soldiers, but as was evident in the Dutch Gap incident in October 1864, it helped to ensure that Confederate officials treated the black prisoners as they wanted their own captured soldiers treated.[1]

Another sign that the Union leadership had begun to gain confidence in black soldiers was the movement toward commissioning African-American officers. None of the blacks in the 5th USCT

would gain officer's straps, but O. S. B. Wall, who had helped recruit the regiment, earned a captain's commission, and John Mercer
Langston, the regiment's chief recruiter, was awaiting confirmation
of his commission as a lieutenant colonel when the war ended.

However, the changes in army life did not mirror changes in
Ohio life. The 5th USCT's return in September 1865 was similar
to its departure. The African-American community welcomed the
men home; the white community took little notice. The press noted
their return and that the African-American community had thrown
the returning troops a picnic, but no general public welcome was
forthcoming.[2]

When the African-American soldiers returned to Ohio, they found
virtually the same conditions they had left. Despite their service and
willingness to participate in the duties of citizens, the black soldiers
soon saw that their neighbors were little more willing to give them
equal legal rights. Ohio, already a free state, had ratified the Thir-
teenth Amendment, which abolished slavery, without opposition.
However, the legislature was less willing to address changes to the
Constitution that affected Ohio law. These were the changes that
the black citizens had vocally sought in the years before and during
the war. Ohio's African Americans wanted the opportunity to vote,
regardless of their racial admixture. The legislature struggled with
granting suffrage to Ohio's blacks. It ratified the Fourteenth Amendment, which granted equal protection under the law, in January
1867, then rescinded its ratification in January 1868.[3]

This turnaround was spurred by a proposed amendment to the
Ohio Constitution that would have granted suffrage to all males
above the age of twenty-one, regardless of color. In a referendum,
the measure was defeated by more than fifty thousand votes, con-
firming the view in the predominantly Democratic state assembly
that Ohio was not ready for universal male suffrage. Consequently,
the assembly initially intended also to refuse to ratify the Fifteenth
Amendment when Congress proposed it in 1869. When it became
apparent that the nation would ratify the amendment without Ohio's
assent, the assembly, fearing possible political ramifications of non-
ratification, approved it by one vote.[4]

What then, was the purpose of the struggle and suffering of Ohio's
African-American men? What cause inspired no fewer than 5,902
men out of a total draft-age population of 7,161 to volunteer for

the war?[5] Clearly the veterans did not enjoy great personal benefits from their service. Quite the opposite is true. These soldiers did not gain great wealth or power, nor did their service create any fundamental change in the minds of Ohio's white population. Those who had been favorably disposed toward African Americans before the war continued to help them and to work with African Americans to achieve their goal of racial equality. Those whose had racial biases against African Americans continued to work against them, inciting the large number of white Ohioans who had no strong feelings either way.

The regiment's soldiers returned to their prewar pursuits. Although some 5th USCT soldiers proposed banding together after the war to help change their status in the state, nothing came of it. The poverty and rural nature of many of the soldiers dictated that they focus their attention on the families they had left behind. Others of the regiment returned home with debilitating injuries and illnesses from their service.

Milton Holland was perhaps the most likely soldier to lead the men in their postwar lives. He had the charisma, intelligence, and abilities to be such a leader. However, he had personal goals to pursue. He left Ohio soon after the war to move to Washington, D.C., where he studied law, served as a department head in the post office, and became involved in banking ventures with Washington luminaries. Holland's home in Silver Spring, Maryland, became a center of black society in the Washington area. When he died, he was buried among many of his USCT comrades in Arlington National Cemetery.

Although the soldiers may not have realized it, the 5th USCT's service united these men with the great tide of social change. They had helped to preserve a union and, in so doing, ensured that the rights of all the Union's citizens took precedence over the racist wishes of any single state. The war did not bring many of them money or social status, but it brought them the opportunity to fight for their race's freedom throughout the country, and it led to their right to vote. With suffrage would come the ability to change the society in which they and their children would live through the generations.

Their struggle was service in the truest sense of the word. The legacy they left was only a beginning, but it was the essential step.

White Ohioans controlled the wealth, the institutions of health and education, and nearly every other facet of Ohio life, but the vote ensured that no longer could the needs of the African-American community be blithely ignored. As the Cincinnati press noted, "Left to themselves, under impartial laws, both whites and blacks, natives and adopted citizens, must work out their own salvation."[6] This opportunity was these soldiers' legacy.

APPENDIX A

USCT Enlistments by State

Free States		Slaveholding	
Pennsylvania	8,612	Louisiana	24,052
Ohio	**5,092**	Kentucky	23,703
New York	4,125	Tennessee	20,133
Massachusetts	3,966	Mississippi	17,869
District of Columbia	3,269	Maryland	8,718
Kansas	2,080	Missouri	8,344
Rhode Island	1,837	Virginia	5,723
Illinois	1,811	Arkansas	5,526
Connecticut	1,764	South Carolina	5,462
Indiana	1,537	North Carolina	5,035
Michigan	1,387	Alabama	4,969
New Jersey	1,185	Georgia	3,486
Iowa	440	Florida	1,044
West Virginia	196	Delaware	954
Wisconsin	165	Texas	47
New Hampshire	125		
Vermont	120		
Minnesota	104		
Maine	104		
Colorado Territory	95		
No state credited	5,896		
Officers	7,122		
Total	51,032	Total	135,065

Source: Adjutant General's Office, Bureau for Colored Troops, *Annual Report, 1865,* October 20, 1865, in U.S. War Department, Adjutant General's Office, *The Negro in the Military Service of the United States, 1639–1877,* reel 4, vol. 6, *1865– 1877,* 3723.

APPENDIX B

Results of Qualifying Examinations

Name	Military Tactics	Military Regulations	General Military Knowledge	Math	History	Geography	Finding	Commissioned as/Highest Rank
Chapin	—	—	P	P	P	P	2LT	2LT/2LT
Johnson, J.F.	P	—	P	Q	Q	P	2LT	2LT/2LT
Jones	—	—	P	P	P	P	2LT	2LT/CPT
Long	P	P	—	Q	—	—	2LT	2LT/2LT
McClelland	P	—	P	P	P	P	2LT	2LT/2LT
Owens	—	—	P	Q	P	P	2LT	2LT/2LT
Spangler	Q	—	P	P	P	P	2LT	2LT/1LT
Viers	P	—	—	P	P	—	2LT	2LT/1LT
Way	P	P	P	P	P	P	2LT	2LT/1LT
Wilson	—	P	P	Q	P	P	2LT	2LT/2LT
Bates	P	P	P	P	P	P	1LT	1LT/CPT
Bennett	P	P	P	Q	Q	P	1LT	1LT/CPT
Griffith	—	—	P	Q	P	P	1LT	1LT/1LT
Johnson	P	P	—	Q	—	—	1LT	1LT/1LT*
Marvin	P	P	P	Q	Q	P	1LT	1LT/BVT MAJ
Price	P	P	P	Q	P	P	1LT	1LT/1LT
Scroggs	P	P	P	P	P	P	1LT	2LT/1LT
Skinner	P	P	P	P	P	P	1LT	1LT/1LT
Smith	P	P	Q	Q	Q	Q	1LT	2LT/1LT*
Stomats	P	P	P	Q	—	P	1LT	1LT/1LT
Wilber	P	P	P	P	P	P	1LT	1LT/CPT
Blood	P	P	P	Q	P	P	CPT	CPT/CPT
Brockway	Q	P	Q	Q	Q	Q	CPT	CPT/CPT
Ford, F.	P	P	P	P	P	P	CPT	CPT/CPT
McCoy	—	P	P	P	P	P	CPT	—/—
Spear	Q	P	P	P	P	P	CPT	CPT/CPT
Cock	P	P	Q	Q	Q	P	MAJ	CPT/CPT
Fahrion	Q	Q	P	Q	Q	P	MAJ	CPT/CPT
Ford, E.	Q	Q	P	Q	Q	P	MAJ	CPT/BVT BG
Oren	P	P	Q	Q	Q	Q	MAJ	CPT/CPT*
Poundstone	P	P	Q	Q	Q	Q	MAJ	CPT/CPT
Terry	P	P	Q	Q	Q	Q	MAJ	MAJ/LTC
Von Heintze	Q	P	P	Q	P	P	MAJ	CPT/CPT
Conine	Q	Q	P	P	P	P	COL	COL/COL

*Officer died while in service.

P=passed

Q=fully qualified

Source: Ohio, Adjutant General's Department, *Report of Candidates Examined for Commissions in Colored Troops, July 18, 1863–February 13, 1864.*

APPENDIX C

5th USCT Officers

Name	Rank	Age	Birthplace	Date Mustered into Regiment	Date Mustered Out and Reason	Co.
James W. Conine	Colonel	36	Conn.	Nov. 20, 1863	Sept. 13, 1864 medical discharge (illness)	Staff
Giles W. Shurtleff	Lieut. Colonel Colonel (Brevet Brigadier General)	32	Canada	July 29, 1863	July 12, 1865 resigned	Staff
John B. Cook	Lieut. Colonel	25	Maine	Oct. 21, 1864	Sept. 20, 1865 mustered out with regiment	Staff
Ira Terry	Major	24	Ohio	Aug. 1, 1863	Sept. 10, 1864 promoted to lt. col. of 22d USCT	Staff
William R. Brazie	Major	28	N.Y.	Oct. 25, 1864	Sept. 20, 1865 mustered out with regiment	Staff
James B. F. Marsh	Regimental	23	Ohio	Aug. 29, 1863	May 17, 1865 resigned	Staff
James L. Patton	Chaplain	36	Ohio	Oct. 29, 1864	May 15, 1865 resigned	Staff
Lyman Allen	Asst. Surgeon, Surgeon	23	Ohio	Oct. 16, 1863	Apr. 22, 1865 resigned	Staff
George V. R. Merrill	Surgeon	24		June 18, 1865	Sept. 20, 1865 mustered out with regiment	Staff
Joseph A. Eastman	Asst. Surgeon	23	N.Y.	Aug. 17, 1865	Sept. 20, 1865 mustered out with regiment	Staff
Henry C. Merryweather	Asst. Surgeon	39	England	Sept. 29, 1863	Apr. 10, 1865 died of disease	Staff
A. Judson Gray	Asst. Surgeon	27		May 6, 1865	Sept. 20, 1865 mustered out with regiment	Staff
Basil S. Spangler	2nd Lieutenant, 1st Lieutenant, Adjutant	20	Ohio	Nov. 14, 1863	Sept. 20, 1865 mustered out with regiment	B, Staff
Orlando Brockway	Captain	28	Ill.	Aug. 21, 1863	June 22, 1864 died of wounds	A
Wales Wilber	1st Lieutenant, Captain	26	Ohio	Sept. 7, 1863	Oct. 17, 1864 died of wounds	F, A

83

Name	Rank	Age	Birthplace	Date Mustered into Regiment	Date Mustered Out and Reason	Co.
Robert H. Jones	2nd Lieutenant, 1st Lieutenant, Captain	22	England	Sept. 25, 1863	Sept. 20, 1865 mustered out with regiment	A
William S. Simmons	2nd Lieutenant	25	R.I.	Nov. 7, 1864	May 15, 1865 medical discharge (wounded)	A
Walter A. Burrows	2nd Lieutenant	25		July 29, 1865	Sept. 20, 1865 mustered out with regiment	A
Karl Von Heintze	Captain	43	France	Aug. 5, 1863	July 29, 1864 dismissed	B
Clifton A. Bennett	1st Lieutenant, Captain	21		Aug. 3, 1863	Sept. 20, 1865 mustered out with regiment	A, B
Henry F. Turner	Adjutant, 1st Lieutenant	20	Ohio	Oct. 9, 1864	Sept. 20, 1865 mustered out with regiment	Staff, B
Robert F. Johnston	1st Lieutenant	30		Nov. 11, 1863	June 15, 1864 killed in action	G, B
Thurston C. Owens	2nd Lieutenant		Ohio	Sept. 4, 1863	Oct. 9, 1863 dismissed	B
Gustavus Fahrion	Captain	24	Germany	Aug. 14, 1863	May 18, 1865 resigned	C
Charles W. Griffith	1st Lieutenant	25	Ohio	Sept. 22, 1863	Oct. 7, 1864 resigned	G, E, C
Peter Stomats	1st Lieutenant	27	Ohio	Sept. 29, 1863	Sept. 3, 1864 resigned	E, C
Alexander M. Poundstone	Captain	28	Ohio	Aug. 20, 1863	Sept. 20, 1865 mustered out with regiment	D
Jacob K. Skinner	1st Lieutenant	28	Ohio	Oct. 7, 1863	April 14, 1864 resigned	D
Lucian Chapin	2nd Lieutenant	22	Ohio	Nov. 16, 1863	May 8, 1865 resigned	D
David L. Way	2nd Lieutenant, 1st Lieutenant	25	Ohio	Nov. 11, 1863	Oct. 12, 1865 mustered out from detached duty	E, D
Charles Oren	Captain	31	Ohio	Aug. 20, 1863	July 28, 1864 killed in action	E
Josiah H. Dearborn	Captain	24	Ohio	Jan. 2, 1865	Sept. 20, 1865 mustered out with regiment	E
Gerard Ramsey	1st Lieutenant	24	Conn.	Aug. 31, 1864	May 3, 1865	E
Oscar E. Doolittle	2nd Lieutenant		Mass.	July 14, 1864	Dec. 19, 1864	E
Ellery C. Ford	Captain	21	Mass.	Sept. 7, 1863	Jan. 27, 1865 promoted to Major, 107th USCT	F

continued

Name	Rank	Age	Birthplace	Date Mustered into Regiment	Date Mustered Out and Reason	Co.
Frank J. Ford	Captain	24	Mass.	Oct. 24, 1863	Sept. 20, 1865 mustered out with regiment	I, E, F
Jacob Bishop	2nd Lieutenant		Vt.	Nov. 7, 1864	May 3, 1865	F
Joseph W. Lone	2nd Lieutenant	26	Ohio	Aug. 24, 1863	Jan. 16, 1864 resigned	F
Jacob T. Johnson	2nd Lieutenant	20	N.Y.	Oct. 1, 1863	Sept. 20, 1865 mustered out with regiment	I, K, F
George B. Cock	Captain	27	Ohio	Sept. 11, 1863	Sept. 20, 1865 mustered out with regiment	G
James B. Johnson	2nd Lieutenant	21	Ill.	Oct. 9, 1864	Jan. 17, 1865 promoted to 1st Lieutenant, 117th USCT	G
Joseph S. McClelland	2nd Lieutenant	26	Penn.	Sept. 30, 1863	Sept. 20, 1865 mustered out with regiment	G
Erastus C. Blood	Captain	28	N.Y.	Oct. 5, 1863	Aug. 28, 1864 resigned	H
Elliott F. Grabill	1st Lieutenant, Adjutant, Captain	26	Ohio	Nov. 19, 1863	Sept. 20, 1865 mustered out with regiment	G, Staff, H
Edwin R. Smith	2nd Lieutenant, 1st Lieutenant	29	N.Y.	Aug. 3, 1863	Aug. 12, 1864 killed in action	H
Frank J. Call	2nd Lieutenant, 1st Lieutenant	19	N.Y.	Oct. 9. 1864	Sept. 20, 1865 mustered out with regiment	C, K, H
Ulysses L. Marvin	1st Lieutenant, Captain (Brevet Major)		Ohio	Aug. 27, 1863	Sept. 20, 1865 mustered out with regiment	I
Albert A. Safford	1st Lieutenant	26	Ohio	Oct. 9, 1864	Sept. 20, 1865 mustered out with regiment	I
David L. Rockwell	2nd Lieutenant		Ohio	June 13, 1865	Sept. 20, 1865 mustered out with regiment	I
Calvin T. Spear	1st Lieutenant, Captain	28	Ohio	Aug. 25, 1863	Aug. 21, 1864 dismissed	H, K
Eugene F. Bates	1st Lieutenant, Captain	21		Nov. 10, 1863	Sept. 20, 1865 mustered out with regiment	B, G, K
John A. Price	1st Lieutenant	23	Mo.	Dec. 31, 1863	Nov. 22, 1864 resigned	K
John B. Viers	2nd Lieutenant, 1st Lieutenant	22	Ohio	Nov. 10, 1863	Sept. 20, 1865 mustered out with regiment	C, F, E, K

Name	Rank	Age	Birthplace	Date Mustered into Regiment	Date Mustered Out and Reason	Co.
Benjamin D. Wilson	2nd Lieutenant	27	Ohio	Feb. 2, 1864	Sept. 13, 1864 resigned	K

Source: United States, War Department, Adjutant General's Office, Service Records, 5th USCT, RG 94, NARA, Washington, D.C.

APPENDIX D

General Orders No. 15

HEADQUARTERS

3d Division, 18th Corps d'Armee

General Orders No. 15   Camp Hamilton, Va., May 1st, 1864

Soldiers of the republic! At last justice has been awarded you by the representatives of the nation in Congress, and you stand before the law upon an equality with your heretofore more favored fellow soldiers of the North.

Induced by no promise of bounty, urged by no consideration of pay, you have taken arms in the cause of your country, prompted only by your patriotism and love of liberty; relying with confidence upon the gratitude and sense of justice of the people, to accord to you the rights that a mistaken polity had withheld.

Your confidence has not been misplaced. By an act that has passed the Senate of the United States, and has been favorably reported to the House of Representatives, you are to be paid hereafter as all other soldiers of the nation are paid.

The General Commanding congratulates you upon this indication of a national appreciation of your worth as soldiers, and recognition of your rights as men, and accounts it an auspicious omen that the initial action of Congress upon this measure was coincident with his assuming command of this Division.

He has carefully observed your soldierly bearing and rapid acquirement of military knowledge. He is conscious that no other regiments in the army are better officered than those of this Division, and he will endeavor to secure a Division organization that shall merit the confidence of this command.

He hopes to lead you soon to victory, and in the hour of triumph we will not visit the wrongs we have suffered upon the persons of the foe, whom the fortunes of war may place in our power, but will be magnanimous to the fallen and humane to the defenceless, offering, if they will receive it, the lesson of humanity due from men.

By command of Brigadier General E. W. Hinks:
SOLON A. CARTER.
Captain and Acting Assistant Adjutant General

APPENDIX E

Prisoners of War

Name	Date Captured	Where Captured	Where Taken and Fate	Co.
Artis, Henry	Sept. 29, 1864	Fort Gilmer	Salisbury, NC, d. Jan. 5, 1865	A
Day, Isaac	Sept. 29, 1864	Fort Gilmer	Richmond Mil Hosp, paroled James River, Va., Feb. 22, 1865	A
Hicks, George	Sept. 29, 1864	Fort Gilmer	Richmond Mil Hosp, d. Oct. 4, 1864	A
Hill, George A.	Sept. 29, 1864	Fort Gilmer	Richmond Mil Hosp, amputee, paroled James River, Va., Feb. 22, 1865	A
James, Benjamin	Sept. 29, 1864	Fort Gilmer	Richmond Mil Hosp, amputee, paroled James River, Va., Feb. 22, 1865	A
Turner, John	Sept. 29, 1864	Fort Gilmer	Richmond Mil Hosp, amputee, d. Oct. 4, 1864	A
Beverly, Samuel	Sept. 29, 1864	Fort Harrison	Salisbury, NC, fate unknown	B
Fortenberry, Daniel	Sept. 29, 1864	Fort Gilmer	Salisbury, NC, d. Jan. 6, 1865	B
Corne, James	Mar. 4, 1864		Andersonville, fate unknown	C
Viers, John	Sept. 29, 1864	Fort Gilmer	Richmond Mil Hosp, paroled City Point, Oct. 9, 1864	
Chafers, John	Sept. 29, 1864	Fort Gilmer	Salisbury, NC, paroled James River, Va., Feb. 22, 1865	D
Good, Thomas	Oct. 27, 1864	Seven Pines	Libby Prison, released to slavemaster, escaped, returned to Regt., Jul. 1, 1865	D
Jordan, Samuel	Dec. 13, 1863	Martinsville, NC	hung by rebels, Dec. 30, 1863	D
Fry, Peyton	May 16, 1864		Salisbury, NC, paroled Northeast Ferry, NC, Mar. 4, 1865	E
Rickman, James	Oct. 27, 1864	Seven Pines	Salisbury, NC, paroled Northeast Ferry, NC, Mar. 4, 1865	E
Taborn, Elias	Oct. 27, 1864	Seven Pines	Salisbury, NC, paroled Northeast Ferry, NC, Mar. 4, 1865	E
Baker, James	May 14, 1864	City Point	Andersonville, paroled Northeast Ferry, NC, Mar. 4, 1865	F
Bowers, William	Sept. 29, 1864	Fort Gilmer	Salisbury, NC, paroled Northeast Ferry, NC, Mar. 4, 1865	F
Cozzens, Whitfield	Sept. 29, 1864	Fort Gilmer	Richmond Mil Hosp, d. Oct. 16, 1864	F
Kennedy, Washington	Sept. 29, 1864	Fort Gilmer	Richmond Mil Hosp, d. Oct. 12, 1864	F
Mabrey, William	Sept. 29, 1864	Fort Gilmer	Richmond Mil Hosp, d. Oct. 11, 1864	F
Shoemaker, William	Sept. 29, 1864	Fort Gilmer	Richmond Mil Hosp, d. Oct. 5, 1864	F
Simpson, John	Sept. 29, 1864	Fort Gilmer	Salisbury, NC, fate unknown	F
Titus, Charles	Sept. 29, 1864	Fort Gilmer	Richmond Mil Hosp, d. Oct. 6, 1864	F
Viney, Calvin	Sept. 29, 1864	Fort Gilmer	Richmond Mil Hosp, d. Oct. 4, 1864	F
Warrick, George	May 14, 1864	City Point	Salisbury, NC, paroled Northeast Ferry, NC, Mar. 4, 1865	F
Wilson, George	Sept. 29, 1864	Fort Gilmer	Salisbury, NC, fate unknown	F

Appendix E

Name	Date Captured	Where Captured	Where Taken and Fate	Co.
Swan, George	May 14, 1864	City Point	Salisbury, NC, paroled Northeast Ferry, NC, Mar. 4, 1865	G
Thomas, Charles	Sept. 29, 1864	Fort Gilmer	Richmond Mil Hosp, d. Oct. 4, 1864	G
Wright, Edward	May 14, 1864	City Point	St. George Courthouse, escaped to Regt.	G
Beard, George	Sept. 29, 1864	Fort Gilmer	Salisbury, NC, paroled Northeast Ferry, NC, Mar. 4, 1865	H
Brown, David	Sept. 29, 1864	Fort Gilmer	released to slavemaster, RC Armistad, d. Nov. 5, 1864	H
Green, Samuel	Sept. 29, 1864	Fort Gilmer	Salisbury, NC, paroled Northeast Ferry, NC, Mar. 4, 1865	H
Lewis, Enoch	Mar. 2, 1864	Bottom Bridge	Goldsboro, NC, paroled Northeast Ferry, NC, Mar. 4, 1865, d. pneumonia Mar. 23, 1865	I
Scott, John	Mar. 5, 1864		fate unknown	I
Whiting, Johnson	Oct. 27, 1864	Seven Pines	Salisbury, NC, paroled Northeast Ferry, NC, Mar. 4, 1865	I
Woods, William	Sept. 29, 1864	Fort Gilmer	Salisbury, NC, fate unknown	K

Source: United States, War Department, Adjutant General's Office, Service Records, 5th USCT, RG 94, NARA, Washington, D.C.

NOTES

Preface

1. John Hope Franklin, *From Slavery to Freedom: A History of American Negroes;* Carter G. Woodson, *The Negro in Our History.*
2. Dudley Taylor Cornish, *The Sable Arm;* John W. Blassingame, "The Union Army as an Educational Institution for Negroes, 1862–1865," and "The Selection of Officers and Non-Commissioned Officers of Negro Troops in the Union Army, 1863–1865"; James M. McPherson, *The Negro's Civil War.*
3. Hondon B. Hargrove, *Black Union Soldiers in the Civil War,* 3.
4. Frederick Douglass, *Douglass' Monthly,* August 1863.
5. See Peter Burchard, *One Gallant Rush: Robert Gould Shaw and His Brave Black Regiment;* Luis F. Emilio, *A Brave Black Regiment: History of the Fifty-fourth Regiment of Massachusetts Volunteer Infantry;* Thomas W. Higginson, *Army Life in a Black Regiment;* Blassingame, "The Union Army as an Educational Institution for Negroes"; Susie Taylor King, *Reminiscences of My Life in Camp.*
6. U.S. War Department, *Official Army Register of the Volunteer Force of the United States Army, 1861–65,* pt. VIII.
7. Cornish, *The Sable Arm,* 316–17.

Chapter 1. Raising the Regiment

1. Fugitive Slave Law of 1850, Dred Scott Case of 1857.
2. Charles H. Wesley, *Ohio Negroes in the Civil War,* 15.
3. *Cleveland Leader,* October 16, 1861.
4. John M. Langston, *From the Virginia Plantation to the National Capitol,* 206. Italics in original.
5. *Christian Recorder* (Philadelphia), August 2, 1862.
6. Ohio Constitution (1802), art. 4, sec. 1: "In all elections all white male inhabitants . . . shall enjoy the right of an elector."
7. Ibid., art. 8, sec. 2.
8. Charles T. Hickok, *The Negro in Ohio, 1802–1870,* 43–44.
9. Ibid., 80–83.
10. Ibid., 54.
11. Joseph T. Glatthaar, *Forged in Battle: The Civil War Alliance of Black Soldiers and White Officers,* 71.
12. *Pine and Palm* (Boston), May 25, 1861.

13. *Liberator* (Boston), May 10, 1861.

14. *Cleveland Leader,* August 13, 1862.

15. Cornish, *The Sable Arm,* 69. Cornish provides an excellent narrative of the events surrounding the recruiting of the 1st Kansas Colored Volunteers. For a brief history of the regiment, see Glenn L. Carle, "The First Kansas Colored."

16. Cornish, *The Sable Arm,* 67. Cornish makes it clear that the original impetus behind the mustering of the Louisiana regiments came not from Butler but from General John Phelps, who resigned in protest of Butler's treatment of the black soldiers. For a discussion of the controversy, see Cornish, 56–68. See also William A. Gladstone, *Men of Color,* 13–14.

17. The texts of the First and Second Confiscation Acts are in United States, *Statutes at Large, Treaties, and Proclamations,* 12: 319, 376–78.

18. Abraham Lincoln, May 19, 1862, in U.S. War Department, comp., *The War of the Rebellion: A Compilation of the Official Records of the Union and Confederate Armies,* ser. 3, vol. 2, p. 43. Hereafter cited as *Official Records.*

19. Cornish, *The Sable Arm,* 50.

20. Wesley, *Ohio Negroes in the Civil War,* 18–21. For a more complete description of the Black Brigade and the situations the African-American community faced during September 1862, see Peter H. Clark, *The Black Brigade of Cincinnati,* and Edgar A. Topping, "Humbly They Served: The Black Brigade in Defense of Cincinnati."

21. In 1860, Massachusetts had a total of only 9,602 African-American men and women of all ages. See U.S. Bureau of the Census, *Negro Population, 1790–1915,* 44. The 54th Massachusetts muster roll listed 156 Ohioans, while the 55th Massachusetts listed 351. See Catherine Wilson, "The 54th and 55th Regiments of Massachusetts Infantry," and Massachusetts Adjutant-General's Office, *Massachusetts Soldiers, Sailors, and Marines in the Civil War,* vol. 4.

22. David Tod to John M. Langston, May 16, 1863 in Ohio, *Message and Reports to the General Assembly and Governor of the State of Ohio for the Year 1863, part I,* 270. Hereafter cited as *1863 Ohio Reports.*

23. David Tod to E. R. Moore and D. E. Fisher, May 16, 1863, David Tod to Reverend J. J. Ward, May 24, 1863, David Tod to Chambers Baird, June 2, 1863, David Tod to Noah L. Wilson, June 9, 1863, all in *1863 Ohio Reports,* 271–73.

24. *Ohio State Journal* (Columbus), May 22, 1863.

25. *Commercial* (Cincinnati), May 13, 1863.

26. *Liberator* (Boston), May 15, 1863.

27. *Cleveland Leader,* April 1, 1863.

28. *Cleveland Leader,* June 25, 1863.

29. Ibid.

30. *Christian Recorder* (Philadelphia), August 16, 1863.

31. *Enquirer* (Cincinnati), July 8, 1863. Emphasis in original.

32. *Crisis* (Columbus), February 25, 1863.

33. Ibid.

34. *Ohio State Journal* (Columbus), July 23, 1863.

35. *Commercial* (Cincinnati), November 9, 1863; Service Records, Wall, O. S. B., 104th USCT, and Holland, Milton, 5th USCT, in U.S. War Department, Adjutant General's Office, Service Records, RG 94, NARA, Washington, D.C.

36. *Herald* (Cleveland), July 24, 1863.

37. *Liberator* (Boston), September 4, 1863.

38. Richard Cain, *Congressional Globe,* 43rd Congress, 1st sess., vol. 2, pt. 1, p. 256, quoted in Wesley, *Ohio Negroes in the Civil War,* 15.

39. *Messenger* (Athens, Ohio), February 4, 1864.

40. U.S. Department of Commerce, *Eighth United States Census, 1860.*

41. Service Record, Holland, Milton, in RG 94, NARA.

42. Ohio Adjutant General's Files, "Muster Rolls, 127th Ohio Volunteer Infantry Regiment (Colored)," OHS, Columbus, Ohio.

43. Service Record, Ivy, George, in RG 94, NARA.

44. The federal government changed nearly all the unit designations for the African-American regiments to USCT regiments. The 127th OVI became the 5th USCT on November 1, 1863. Seven regiments retained their original state designations. See Gladstone, *Men of Color.*

45. Wesley, *Ohio Negroes in the Civil War,* 26, 41.

Chapter 2. Leaders

1. Giles Shurtleff to Mary Burton, June 26, 1863, in Letters sent by GWS, GWS Papers, 1846–1930, OCA, Oberlin, Ohio.

2. Giles Shurtleff to Mary Burton, July 6, 1863, in Letters sent by GWS, GWS Papers.

3. John M. Langston to Major George L. Stearns, October 16, 1863, in U.S. War Department, Adjutant General's Office, Documents, box 12, RG 94, NARA.

4. Ohio Adjutant General's Department, *Report of Candidates Examined for Commissions in Colored Troops, July 18, 1863–February 13, 1864,* OHS, Columbus, Ohio. Hereafter cited as *Report of Examinations.*

5. Giles Shurtleff to Mary E. Burton, July 25, 1863, in Letters sent by GWS, GWS Papers.

6. Ibid.

7. *Report of Examinations.* See Appendix B, Results of Qualifying Examinations.

8. *Journal* (Louisville, Ky.), November 30, 1863, quoted in Cornish, *The Sable Arm,* 223.

9. Giles Shurtleff to Mary Burton, June 18, 1863, in Letters sent by GWS, GWS Papers.

10. Giles Shurtleff to Mary Burton, June 26, 1863.

11. Service Records, Allen, Lyman, and Patton, James, in RG 94, NARA.

12. Giles Shurtleff to Mary Burton, January 10, 1864, in Letters sent by GWS, GWS Papers.

13. First Lt. Charles Williams, Brigade Adjutant, to D. T. Wells, Corps Muster Officer, June 29, 1864, and Service Record, Brown, Jr., both in RG 94, NARA.

14. The Oberlin-Wellington Rescue occurred on September 13, 1858. Slave hunters from Kentucky kidnapped John Price, a black man living in Oberlin, and tried to escape south with him. A crowd of men from Oberlin overtook the Kentuckians in Wellington and freed Price in violation of the Fugitive Slave Law of 1850. Patton tried talking the slave hunters out of their plan. While he had their attention, other men made off with Price. The subsequent trials of the rescuers presented the Buchanan administration with an opportunity to uphold the Fugitive Slave Law. See Nat Brandt, *The Town that Started the Civil War.*

15. U.S. War Department, Adjutant General's Office, "General Orders 114, Headquarters, 2nd Division, 18th Corps," November 14, 1864, and Service Record, Allen, Lyman, both in RG 94, NARA.

16. Lyman Allen to Lieutenant Colonel D. A. Campbell, Acting Adjutant General, April 4, 1865, Giles Shurtleff to Captain S. A. Carter, March 5, 1865, and Service Record, Allen, Lyman, all in RG 94, NARA.

17. Giles Shurtleff to Mary Burton, February 14, 1864, in Letters sent by GWS, GWS Papers.

18. Ohio Adjutant General Files, "Muster Rolls, 127th Ohio Volunteer Infantry Regiment (Colored)."

19. Colonel James Conine to Major R. S. Dennis, August 5, 1864, in U.S. War Department, Adjutant General's Office, Documents, box 12, RG 94, NARA.

20. Major Ira Terry, endorsement to Karl Von Heintze's letter of resignation, July 3, 1864, in Service Record, Von Heintze, Karl, RG 94, NARA.

21. Captain Karl Von Heintze to Major General Benjamin Butler, March 25, 1864, and Lyman Allen, Surgeon's Certificate, n.d., in Service Record, Von Heintze, Karl, RG 94, NARA.

22. Colonel Alonzo Draper, endorsement of letter from Lieutenant Colonel Giles Shurtleff to Major General Ord, September 25, 1864, in Service Record, Fahrion, Gustave, RG 94, NARA.

23. Giles Shurtleff to Mary Burton, July 17, 1864, in Letters sent by GWS, GWS Papers; Giles Shurtleff, endorsement to letter of resignation from Captain Gustave Fahrion to MG John Gibbon, in Service Record, Fahrion, Gustave, RG 94, NARA.

24. Major William R. Brazie to Lieutenant Colonel EW, in U.S. War Department, Adjutant General's Office, Documents, box 12, RG 94, NARA; "Gustave Fahrion" (photostatic copy), Fahrion Papers, private collection of Allan Millett, Columbus, Ohio. Fahrion borrowed a total of $197 from six soldiers and collected $14 in deceased soldiers' pay.

25. Colonel A. C. Vons to Captain Brampton Ives, AAG, 3rd Division, New Berne, N.C., January 9, 1862, and Service Record, Fahrion, Gustave, 67th Ohio Volunteer Infantry, both in RG 94, NARA.

Chapter 3. Training a Regiment for War

1. *Ohio State Journal* (Columbus), July 27, November 5, 1863.
2. Giles W. Shurtleff to Mary E. Burton, September 14, 1863, in Letters sent by GWS, GWS Papers.
3. "5th United States Colored Troops, Special Orders 2—Revision to Schedule," U.S. War Department, Adjutant General's Office, Documents, box 12, RG 94, NARA.
4. Giles W. Shurtleff to Mary E. Burton, August 12, 1863, in Letters sent by GWS, GWS Papers.
5. Giles W. Shurtleff to Mary E. Burton, October 7, 1863, September 14, 1863, in Letters sent by GWS, GWS Papers.
6. Giles Shurtleff to Mary E. Burton, October 5, 1863, ibid.
7. Joel Spears to his sister, October 9, 1863, in U.S. Veterans Administration, Pension Files, Spears, Joel, RG 15, NARA.
8. Giles W. Shurtleff to Mary E. Burton, September 14, 1863, October 7, 1863.
9. Giles W. Shurtleff to Mary E. Burton, September 14, 1863.
10. Giles Shurtleff to Mary E. Burton, September 17, 1863, in Letters sent by GWS, GWS Papers. Owens's family viewed his dismissal as a family disgrace. In a letter that Owens wrote to Lieutenant Colonel Shurtleff, he begged the colonel to review his case so that he might enlist as a private to restore his family's honor. He attributed his father's death on the shame his son's dismissal had brought to his family. See Thurston Owens to Giles Shurtleff, February 26, 1864, in Letters received by GWS, 1863–1865, GWS Papers.
11. Service Records: Carter, Isaac; Goings, Braxton; Haden, William; Harrison, William; Henry, Charles; Malone, Archie; McCorgin, John; McCorgin, Reuben; Moore, William; Palmer, Jonah; Payne, John; Pettiford, John; Wagoner, Ephraim; Warren, Louis; Wheeler, Charles; Wyatt, Ira, 5th USCT, in RG 94, NARA; Giles W. Shurtleff to Mary E. Burton, September 22, 1863, in Letters sent by GWS, GWS Papers; Whitelaw Reid, *Ohio in the War: Her Statesmen, Her Generals, and Soldiers,* vol. 2, *The History of Her Regiments and Other Military Organizations.* Allen later faced charges of gross negligence. He resigned rather than face a review board to judge his competence.
12. *Daily Gazette* (Cincinnati), November 12, 1863; *Gazette* (Delaware, Ohio), November 13, 1863.
13. *Daily Gazette* (Cincinnati), November 12, 1863.

Chapter 4. The Regiment Moves South

1. Colonel James Conine to Brigadier General Edward Wild, November 29, 1863, in U.S. War Department, Adjutant General's Office, Documents, box 12, RG 94, NARA.
2. Giles W. Shurtleff to Mary Burton, November 19, December 4, 1863, in Letters sent by GWS, GWS Papers.

3. Regimental Return, November 30, 1863, in U.S. War Department, Adjutant General's Office, Documents, box 5330, RG 94, NARA.

4. *Messenger* (Athens, Ohio), February 4, 1864; Brigadier General Wild to Brigadier General James Barnes, December 12, 1863, in *Official Records,* ser. 1, vol. 29, pt. 2, p. 562.

5. Service Record, Corne, James W., in RG 94, NARA.

6. BG Wild to BG Getty, December 4, 1863, BG Getty to BG Wild, December 6, 1863, BG Wild to BG James Barnes, December 12, 1863, all in *Official Records,* ser. 1, vol. 29, pt. 2, pp. 542–43, 562.

7. Major General George Pickett to General Samuel Cooper, December 15, 1863, ibid., 872–73.

8. Giles W. Shurtleff to Mary E. Burton, December 25, 1863, in Letters sent by GWS, GWS Papers. Shurtleff describes the event in graphic detail, including his own attempts to bring the prisoner to repentance before "the poor deluded soul was hurled into eternity all unprepared."

9. Captain George Cock to Brigadier General L. Thomas, December 29, 1863, in U.S. War Department, Adjutant General's Office, Documents, box 12, RG 94, NARA.

10. *Messenger* (Athens, Ohio), February 4, 1864.

11. Giles W. Shurtleff to Mary Burton, January 14, February 4, 1864, in Letters sent by GWS, GWS Papers.

12. 5th Regiment, USCT, Morning Report, February 13, 1864, in U.S. War Department, Adjutant General's Office, Documents, box 5331, Morning Reports, Cos. A to K, RG 94, NARA.

13. Field and Staff Muster Roll, April 30, 1864, in U.S. War Department, Adjutant General's Office, Documents, box 5330, RG 94, NARA.

14. Giles Shurtleff to Mary Burton, January 10, 1864. Emphasis in original.

15. James Conine to Major G. W. Foster, February 27, 1864, in U.S. War Department, Adjutant General's Office, Documents, box 12, RG 94, NARA.

16. Giles W. Shurtleff to Mary Burton, February 11, 1864, in Letters sent by GWS, GWS Papers. The other infantry regiments involved were the 118th, 139th, and 148th New York, 25th Massachusetts, and 4th and 6th USCT.

17. Joseph J. Scroggs, entries for March 1–5, 1864, in Diary, 1864–65, pts. 1 and 2 (photostat), *Civil War Times Illustrated* Collection, U.S. Army Military History Institute, Carlisle Barracks, Pennsylvania.

18. Robert M. West to Major General Butler, March 4, 1864, in *Official Records,* ser. 1, vol. 33, pp. 198, 240–44, 671.

19. See Glatthaar, *Forged in Battle,* 170; General Order 163, Adjutant General's Office, June 4, 1863, in *Official Records,* ser. 3, vol. 3, p. 252.

20. "Wild Jack," letter to the editor, July 28, 1864, in *Christian Recorder* (Philadelphia), August 6, 1864.

21. Scroggs, Diary, 1864–65, entry for March 30, 1864.

22. See Glatthaar, *Forged in Battle,* chap. 9; also see Appendix D, General Orders No. 15.

23. The Fort Pillow massacre, which occurred on April 12, 1864, remains one of the most infamous of Civil War atrocities. Two-thirds of the 262

African-American soldiers died, and about one-third of the 295 white Union soldiers lost their lives, many after they had attempted to surrender. See John Cimprich and Robert C. Mainfort Jr., "Fort Pillow Revisited: New Evidence about an Old Controversy"; Hargrove, *Black Union Soldiers in the Civil War;* Giles W. Shurtleff to Mary Burton, April 17, 1864, in Letters sent by GWS, GWS Papers.

24. Giles W. Shurtleff to Mary Burton, April 28, 1864, in Letters sent by GWS, GWS Papers.

25. Special Orders 113, April 23, 1864, Troops in the Department of Virginia and North Carolina, April 30, 1864, *Official Records,* ser. 1, vol. 33, pp. 957, 1053–58. The April 30 list refers to the unit as the "Division U. S. Colored Troops."

26. Giles W. Shurtleff to Mary Burton, May 12, 1864, in Letters sent by GWS, GWS Papers.

27. *Official Records,* ser. 1, vol. 36, pt. 1, p. 118.

28. Giles W. Shurtleff to Mary Burton, May 17, 1864, in Letters sent by GWS, GWS Papers.

29. Service Records: Baker, James P.; Warrick, George; Swan, George, in RG 94, NARA.

30. Service Record, Fry, Peyton, ibid.; Giles Shurtleff to Mary Burton, May 23, 1864, in Letters sent by GWS, GWS Papers.

31. Samuel A. Duncan, Report, June 25, 1864, in *Official Records,* ser. 1, vol. 51, pt. 1, pp. 265–69.

32. P. G. T. Beauregard, "Four Days of Battle at Petersburg," in *Battles and Leaders,* ed. Robert U. Johnson and Clarence C. Buel, 4:541.

33. Duncan, Report, June 25, 1864.

34. E. W. Hinks to Major General W. F. Smith, June 27, 1864, in *Official Records,* ser. 1, vol. 40, pt. 2, pp. 490–91.

35. *Crisis* (Columbus), June 22, 1864.

36. Giles Shurtleff to Mary E. Burton, June 26, 1864, in Letters sent by GWS, GWS Papers.

37. Tri-monthly Consolidated Morning Report, Fifth United States Colored Troops, July 19, 1864, in U.S. War Department, Adjutant General's Office, Documents, box 12, RG 94, NARA.

38. James M. McPherson, *Battle Cry of Freedom,* 741.

39. *Messenger* (Athens, Ohio), August 4, 1864. According to the AGO files, nine of the soldiers of C Company were dead by the time Sergeant Holland wrote. Because months would pass before soldiers returned from the hospital, it is very likely that he was unaware of four of the deaths. The remaining soldier, Abraham Scott, died of measles while still at Camp Delaware.

40. Tri-monthly Consolidated Morning Report, Fifth United States Colored Troops, July 19, 1864.

41. Giles Shurtleff to Mary E. Burton, July 8, 1864, in Letters sent by GWS, GWS Papers.

42. Giles Shurtleff to Mary E. Burton, July 21, 1864, ibid.; Elliott Grabill, letter to the editor, June 30, 1864, in *Lorain County News* (Oberlin), July 20, 1864.

43. Elliott F. Grabill, letter to the editor, July 29, 1864, in *Lorain County News* (Oberlin), August 17, 1864.

44. Dillon Chavers to Sarah Oren, November 24, 1864, in *Dearest Sattie: Civil War Letters of Capt. Charles Oren, 5th U.S.C.T.,* ed. Oren, 99.

45. *Lorain County News* (Oberlin, Ohio), August 24, 1864. See also Robert S. Fletcher, *A History of Oberlin College from Its Foundation through the Civil War,* 852–63.

46. Tri-monthly Consolidated Morning Report, Fifth United States Colored Troops, July 19, 1864.

47. Giles Shurtleff to Mary E. Burton, August 5, 1864, in Letters sent by GWS, GWS Papers. The 36th USCT previously had been designated 2nd North Carolina Colored Volunteers. The 38th was a Virginia regiment. Lieutenant Colonel Shurtleff's supposition was incorrect. The day after he wrote to Mary Burton, he received a letter from Colonel Samuel Duncan, who remained in command of the 3rd Brigade, 3rd Division, XVIII Army Corps. Colonel Duncan explained that General Paine, the division commander, had not taken personalities into account but had simply placed the commanders into three groups of three based on their seniority. He then matched the senior officer of the first group with the junior member of the second group and the center member of the third group. In this way, he hoped to field three equally well-led brigades.

48. Thomas M. Chester, dispatch to the Philadelphia *Press,* September 1, 1864, in *Thomas Morris Chester, Black Civil War Correspondent: His Dispatches from the Virginia Front,* ed. R. J. M. Blackett, 115.

49. Ibid., 118–19; Pension File, Blood, Erastus, RG 15, NARA. While Captain Blood was a poor officer, he may not demonstrate a failure of the qualifying examination idea. Colonel Samuel Duncan's endorsement of his resignation noted that "Capt. Blood himself has said that he owes his present position in the regiment to the favoritism of a member of the Cincinnati Board, who gave him a thorough insight into the course of examination to which he would be subjected."

50. Giles Shurtleff to Major R. S. Davis, August 28, 1864, in U.S. War Department, Adjutant General's Office, Documents, box 5330, RG 94, NARA.

51. Of these officers, only Captain Fahrion was not discharged from the service.

52. Giles Shurtleff to Mary Burton, August 29, 1864, in Letters sent by GWS, GWS Papers. The Confederate 4th Texas Regiment was the rebel force. This force also enjoyed the brief respite from the constant sniping. One Texan remarked that they were "not grumbling at the task either—the darkies, so far, appearing devoid of beligerent [sic] propensities" (Joseph B. Polley, *A Soldier's Letters to Charming Nellie,* 249).

53. Richard J. Sommers, *Richmond Redeemed: The Siege at Petersburg,* covers the subject of Grant's fifth offensive in exhaustive detail.

54. Giles Shurtleff to John Brough, August 29, 1864 (telegram), in Letters sent by GWS, GWS Papers; John Brough to Giles Shurtleff, September 3,

1864, in Letters received by GWS, GWS Papers; C. W. Foster to J. H. Potter, in U.S. War Department, Adjutant General's Office, *The Negro in the Military Service of the United States, 1639–1886,* reel 3, vols. 4–5, *1864,* 2, 773.

55. Giles Shurtleff to Major C. W. Worth, August 9, 1864, 1LT Edward Hughes to Captain Fred Martin, October 29, 1864, in U.S. War Department, Adjutant General's Office, Documents, box 5330, RG 94, NARA.

Chapter 5. The Battle of New Market Heights and Aftermath

1. Sommers, *Richmond Redeemed,* 2–4.

2. Ibid., 4–5.

3. Giles W. Shurtleff, "Reminiscences, 1881," in Writings re the Civil War, GWS Papers.

4. Elliott Grabill to Anna Grabill, September 30, 1864, in Elliott Grabill Papers, 1859–1910, OCA, Oberlin, Ohio.

5. Sommers, *Richmond Redeemed,* 30–38; Elliott Grabill to Anna Grabill, September 30, 1864; Elliott Grabill, letter to the editor, October 2, 1864, in *Lorain County News* (Oberlin, Ohio), October 19, 1864.

6. Henry Peck, letter to the editor, in *Lorain County News* (Oberlin), October 12, 1864.

7. Giles Shurtleff to Mary Burton, October 23, 1864, in Letters sent by GWS, GWS Papers; *Official Records,* ser. 1, vol. 42, pt. 3, p. 168. Although Bronson, Beatty, and Pinn lived out their lives in relative obscurity, Milton Holland became a prominent lawyer, administrator, and banker in Washington, D.C. See Jennifer Johnson, ed., *Milton M. Holland: Panola County Recipient of the Medal of Honor.*

8. Benjamin Butler, quoted in "General Shurtleff," by Ulysses Marvin, *Oberlin Alumni Magazine,* 321.

9. Scroggs, Diary, 1864–1865, entry for September 29, 1864.

10. Sommers, *Richmond Redeemed,* 38.

11. Ibid., 58; George Rogers, "Will Colored Troops Fight?" *Ohio State Journal* (Columbus), July 27, 1864.

12. Elliott Grabill to Anna Grabill, September 30, 1864; Elliott Grabill to Giles Shurtleff, in Letters received by GWS, GWS Papers; "The Conduct and Casualties of the 5th U. S. Colored Troops in the Late Battle near Richmond," *Lorain County News* (Oberlin, Ohio), October 12, 1864.

13. Service Records: Artis, Henry; Beard, George; Beverly, Samuel; Bowers, William; Brown, David; Chafers, John; Cozzens, Whitfield; Day, Isaac; Fortenberry, Daniel; Green, Samuel; Hicks, George; Hill, George A.; James, Benjamin; Kennedy, Washington; Mabrey, William; Shoemaker, William; Simpson, John; Thomas, Charles; Titus, Charles; Turner, John; Viney, Calvin; Wilson, George; and Woods, William, in RG 94, NARA.

14. *National Anti-Slavery Standard* (New York), October 22, 1864.

15. Benjamin Butler to Robert Ould, August 1864, in U.S. War Department, Adjutant General's Office, *The Negro in the Military Service,* reel 5,

vol. 7, *Treatment and Exchange of Prisoners of War* [hereafter cited as *Treatment of Prisoners*], 4339–51. Illustrative of the Union leadership's resolve is a letter from Union officers held prisoner in Charleston. These men pleaded with President Lincoln to resume the prisoner exchanges regardless of what happened to the black soldiers because while "it is true they are again made slaves, . . . their slavery is freedom and justice compared with the cruel existence imposed upon our gallant men." The president did not waver in the face of even such an impassioned plea. Blackett, *Thomas Morris Chester,* 142–43, 147.

16. M. P. Turner to W. H. Hatch, October 14, 1864, Richard Ewell to M. P. Turner, October 5, 1864, in *Treatment of Prisoners,* 4653b, 4655a.

17. Benjamin Butler to Robert Ould, October 12, 1864; Benjamin Butler to Robert Ould, October 13, 1864, with endorsement by General U. S. Grant: "I have approved of the retaliatory measures proposed by Gen. Butler and accordingly sent to Dutch Gap this evening all the prisoners of war now with this army"; Benjamin Butler, General Order 126, Headquarters, Department of Virginia and North Carolina, October 13, 1864; Robert E. Lee to Ulysses S. Grant, October 19, 1864; Benjamin Butler, General Order 134, Headquarters, Department of Virginia and North Carolina, October 20, 1864, in *Treatment of Prisoners,* 4366, 4368, 4370, 4379, 4654–55.

18. *Official Records,* ser. 1, vol. 42, pt. 1, p. 163.

19. Major General Benjamin Butler, October 11, 1864, *Official Records,* ser. 1, vol. 42, pt. 3, p. 163.

20. Ibid., 168. The four orderly sergeants received their Medals of Honor April 6, 1865 (Elliott Grabill to Giles Shurtleff, October 23, 1864, in Letters received by GWS, GWS Papers). The silver medal that Butler commissioned in honor of the colored soldiers was the Army of the James medal. Gladstone states that only 197 medals—the only medal struck for colored troops—were made (Gladstone, *Men of Color,* 150).

21. Quartermaster Records, 5th USCT, October 29, 1864, in U.S. War Department, Adjutant General's Office, RG 94, NARA.

22. Scroggs, Diary, 1864–65, entry for October 6–8, 1864.

23. Ibid., October 8, 1864; Blackett, *Thomas Morris Chester,* 171.

24. Giles Shurtleff to Mary Burton, October 26, 28, 1864, in Letters sent by GWS, GWS Papers.

25. Blackett, *Thomas Morris Chester,* 149–50; Giles Shurtleff to Mary Burton, October 26, 1864.

26. *Official Records,* ser. 1, vol. 42, pt. 3, pp. 365–68.

27. Ibid., p. 399; *Official Records,* ser. 1, vol. 42, pt. 1, pp. 814–17; Scroggs, Diary, 1864–65, entry for October 27, 1864; Service Record, Ryder, William, in RG 94, NARA. Although Ryder survived the wound, his wartime experience was finished. He returned to Oberlin, where he completed his degree and became a Congregationalist pastor and doctor of divinity at Harvard.

28. *Laws of Ohio* 2:5; Hickok, *The Negro in Ohio,* 44; Blackett, *Thomas Morris Chester,* 188–89; *Lorain County News* (Oberlin, Ohio), December 7, 1864.

29. *Lorain County News* (Oberlin, Ohio), December 7, 1864.

Chapter 6. Operations in North Carolina, 1864–1865

1. U.S. War Department, General Order 297, December 3, 1964, *Official Records,* ser. 1, vol. 42, pt. 3, p. 791.
2. Rod Gragg, *Confederate Goliath: The Battle of Fort Fisher,* 11–12.
3. Ulysses S. Grant to Benjamin Butler, December 6, 1864, in *Official Records,* ser. 1, vol. 42, pt. 3, p. 835.
4. Gragg, *Confederate Goliath,* 43–44.
5. Scroggs, Diary, 1864–65, entries for December 16–18, 1864; Giles Shurtleff to Mary Shurtleff, December 18, 21, 1864, in Letters sent by GWS, GWS Papers.
6. Scroggs, Diary, 1864–65, entry for December 25, 1864.
7. Benjamin Butler to Rear Admiral David Porter, December 25, 1864, in *Official Records,* ser. 1, vol. 42, pt. 3, pp. 1,075–76.
8. Giles Shurtleff to Mary Shurtleff, January 2, 1865, in Letters sent by GWS, GWS Papers; "Another Letter from the Army in Virginia," *Lorain County News* (Oberlin, Ohio), February 22, 1865.
9. Giles Shurtleff to Mary Shurtleff, January 20, 1865, in Letters sent by GWS, GWS Papers.
10. James M. Merrill, "The Fort Fisher and Wilmington Campaign: Letters from Rear Admiral David D. Porter," *North Carolina Historical Review* 35, no. 4 (1958): 468.
11. Scroggs, Diary, 1864–65, entries for January 9–13, 1865.
12. Braxton Bragg, January 20, 1865, *Official Records,* ser. 1, vol. 46, pt. 1, p. 433.
13. "Letter from Capt. Grabill," in *Lorain County News* (Oberlin, Ohio), March 8, 1865.
14. "Letter from Capt. Grabill," *Lorain County News* (Oberlin, Ohio), March 15, 1865.
15. Ibid.
16. Brigadier General Charles Paine, April 24, 1865, *Official Records,* ser. 1, vol. 47, pt. 1, pp. 924–26.
17. Scroggs, Diary, 1864–65, entries for February 22-March 8, 1865.
18. Giles Shurtleff to Mary Shurtleff, March 29, 1865, in Letters sent by GWS, GWS Papers.
19. Giles Shurtleff to Mary Shurtleff, February 12, 1865, ibid.
20. Scroggs, Diary, 1864–65, entries for March 17-April 20, 1865.
21. Giles Shurtleff to Mary Shurtleff, May 2, 1865, in Letters sent by GWS, GWS Papers.
22. Giles Shurtleff to Mary Shurtleff, May 19, 1865, ibid.
23. Ibid.
24. Scroggs, Diary, 1864–65, entry for January 2, 1865; Giles Shurtleff to Mary Shurtleff, February 6, May 19, 1865, in Letters sent by GWS, GWS Papers.
25. "Grabill Still in the Army," *Lorain County News* (Oberlin, Ohio), June 14, 1865.
26. Giles Shurtleff to Mary Burton, June 18, 1863; Giles Shurtleff to Mary Shurtleff, May 9, 24, 1865, in Letters sent by GWS, GWS Papers. Shurtleff

left the regiment to begin teaching at Oberlin College. His position as a tutor paid him $50 per month. As a regimental commander, he was earning $240 per month.

27. Giles Shurtleff, farewell speech, June 24, 1865, copy in U.S. War Department, Adjutant General's Office, Documents, box 5330, RG 94, NARA.

28. Service Record, Cook, John, in RG 94, NARA.

29. 5th USCT, General Order 7, July 26, 1865, and 5th USCT, General Order 8, August 16, 1865, in U.S. War Department, Adjutant General's Office, Documents, box 5330, RG 94, NARA.

30. 5th USCT, Morning Report, September 19, 1865, in U.S. War Department, Adjutant General's Office, Documents, box 5330, Cos. A through K, RG 94, NARA.

31. Service Records, 5th USCT, in RG 94, NARA.

32. John P. Davis, ed., *The American Negro Reference Book*, 613.

33. Dyer, Frederick, *A Compendium of the War of the Rebellion*, quoted in William A. Gladstone, *United States Colored Troops, 1863–1867*, 118. See also Frederick Phisterer, *Statistical Record of the Armies of the United States*. Phisterer shows that USCT soldiers were only half as likely to be sick in the hospital and absent but were almost twice as likely to die, even though battle losses were nearly equal.

Chapter 7. Conclusion

1. See *Negro Military Service* for the documents describing both sides of the Civil War prisoner conflict, the reasons for the breakdown of the cartel, and the events surrounding the use of Confederate prisoners in the Dutch Gap Canal.

2. *Ohio State Journal* (Columbus), October 8, 1865.

3. *Laws of Ohio*, 64:320, 65:280, quoted in Hickok, *The Negro in Ohio*, 72.

4. Hickok, *The Negro in Ohio*, 75.

5. Wesley, *Ohio Negroes in the Civil War*, 26, 41. The population figure is for African-American men between eighteen and forty-five in 1860. The figure for the number who served from Ohio does not count the soldiers who enlisted in Massachusetts regiments (estimated at over 900) or any of the 99,337 recruits not credited to any state.

6. *Commercial* (Cincinnati), April 15, 1870.

BIBLIOGRAPHY

Primary Sources

Official Documents

Massachusetts. Adjutant-General's Office. *Massachusetts Soldiers, Sailors, and Marines in the Civil War.* Vol. 4. Norwood, Mass.: Norwood Press, 1932.

Ohio. Adjutant General Files. "Muster rolls, 127th Ohio Volunteer Infantry Regiment (Colored)." Ohio Historical Society, Columbus, Ohio.

Ohio. Adjutant General's Department. *Report of Candidates Examined for Commissions in Colored Troops, July 18, 1863–February 13, 1864.* Ohio Historical Society, Columbus, Ohio.

Ohio. *Message and Reports to the General Assembly and Governor of the State of Ohio for the Year 1863, part I.* Columbus, Ohio: Richard Nevins, State Printer, 1864.

United States. Bureau of the Census. *Negro Population, 1790–1915.* Washington, D.C.: Government Printing Office, 1918. Reprint, New York: Kraus Reprint, 1969.

United States. Department of Commerce. *Eighth United States Census, 1860.* Ohio Historical Society, Columbus, Ohio.

United States. *Statutes at Large, Treaties, and Proclamations.* Vol. 12. Boston: Little, Brown, 1863.

United States. Veterans Administration. Pension Files. RG 15. NARA, Washington, D.C.

United States. War Department. Adjutant General's Office. Documents. Box 12, Regimental Papers 3rd–5th U.S. Colored Inf. RG 94. NARA, Washington, D.C.

———. Adjutant General's Office. Documents. Box 5330, Volunteer Organizations, Civil War, United States Colored Troops, 5th Infantry Field and Staff. RG 94. NARA, Washington, D.C.

———. Adjutant General's Office. Documents. Box 5331, Volunteer Organizations, Civil War, United States Colored Troops, 5th Infantry, 6th Infantry. RG 94. NARA, Washington, D.C.

———. Adjutant General's Office. *The Negro in the Military Service of the United States, 1639–1886.* 7 vols. Washington, D.C.: National Archives and Records Administration Service, 1963. NARA microform. 5 reels.

———. Adjutant General's Office. Service Records. RG 94. NARA, Washington, D.C.

———. *Official Army Register of the Volunteer Force of the United States Army, 1861–65.* Part VIII. Washington, D.C., 1867.

———, comp. *The War of the Rebellion: A Compilation of the Official Records of the Union and Confederate Armies.* Washington, D.C.: Government Printing Office, 1880–1901.

Newspapers

Christian Recorder (Philadelphia). August 2, 1862; August 16, 1863; August 6, 1864.

Commercial (Cincinnati, Ohio). May 13, November 9, 1863; April 15, 1870.

Crisis (Columbus, Ohio). February 25, 1863; June 22, 1864.

Daily Gazette (Cincinnati, Ohio). November 12, 1863.

Douglass' Monthly (Philadelphia). August 1863.

Enquirer (Cincinnati, Ohio). July 8, 1863.

Herald (Cleveland). July 24, 1863.

Gazette (Delaware, Ohio). November 13, 1863.

Journal (Louisville, Ky.). November 30, 1863.

Leader (Cleveland). October 16, 1861; August 13, 1862; April 1, June 25, 1863.

Liberator (Boston). May 10, 1861; May 15, September 4, 1863.

Lorain County News (Oberlin, Ohio). July 20, August 17, 24, October 12, 19, December 7, 1864; February 22, March 8, 15, June 14, 1865.

Messenger (Athens, Ohio). February 4, August 4, 1864.

National Anti-Slavery Standard (New York). October 22, 1864.

Ohio State Journal (Columbus). May 22, July 23, 27, November 5, 1863; July 27, 1864; October 8, 1865.

Pine and Palm (Boston). May 25, 1861.

Unpublished

Fahrion, Gustave. Papers. Private collection of Allen Millett, Columbus, Ohio.

Grabill, Elliot. Papers. 1859–1910. Oberlin College Archives, Oberlin, Ohio.

Scroggs, Joseph J. Diary, 1864–65, 5th U.S. Colored Troops. Parts 1 and 2 (photostat). *Civil War Times Illustrated* Collection. U.S. Army Military History Institute, Carlisle Barracks, Pennsylvania.

————. Diary, 1861–63, 104th Ohio Infantry Regiment. Part 1 [photostat]. *Civil War Times Illustrated* Collection. U.S. Army Military History Institute, Carlisle Barracks, Pennsylvania.

Shurtleff, Giles Waldo. Papers. 1846–1930. Oberlin College Archives, Oberlin, Ohio.

Spears, Joel. Letter dated October 9, 1863, to his sister. United States. Veterans Administration. Pension Files—Spears, Joel. RG 15, NARA, Washington, D.C.

Tod, David. Letter dated July 17, 1863, to Captain Lewis McCoy. Adjutant General's Papers, Ohio Archives, Ohio Historical Society, Columbus, Ohio.

Published

Berlin, Ira, Joseph P. Reidy, and Leslie Rowland, eds. *The Black Military Experience.* Series II, *Freedom: A Documentary History of Emancipation, 1861–1867.* Cambridge: Cambridge University Press, 1982.

Beauregard, P. G. T. "Four Days of Battle at Petersburg." In *Battles and Leaders.* Vol. 4. Edited by Robert U. Johnson and Clarence C. Buel. New York: The Century Company, 1884.

Chester, Thomas Morris. *Thomas Morris Chester, Black Civil War Correspondent: His Dispatches from the Virginia Front.* Edited by R. J. M. Blackett. Baton Rouge: Louisiana State University Press, 1989.

Dyer, Frederick. *A Compendium of the War of the Rebellion.* 2 vols. Dayton, Ohio: Morningside Bookshop, 1908.

Nalty, Bernard C., and Morris J. MacGregor, eds. *Blacks in the Military: Essential Documents.* Wilmington, Del.: Scholarly Resources, 1981.

Oren, Timothy, ed. *Dearest Sattie: Civil War Letters of Capt. Charles Oren, 5th U.S.C.T.* Dublin, Ohio: Timothy Oren, 1995.

Polley, Joseph B. *A Soldier's Letters to Charming Nellie.* New York: Neale Publishing Co., 1908.

Reid, Whitelaw. *Ohio in the War: Her Statesmen, Her Generals, and Soldiers*. Vol. 2, *The History of Her Regiments and Other Military Organizations*. Cincinnati: Moore, Wilstach, and Baldwin, 1868.

Secondary Sources

Books

Bigglestone, William E. *They Stopped in Oberlin: Black Residents and Visitors of the Nineteenth Century*. Scottsdale, Ariz.: Innovation Group, 1981.

Brandt, Nat. *The Town that Started the Civil War*. Syracuse: Syracuse University Press, 1990.

Brown, William W. *The Negro in the American Rebellion*. 1867. Reprint, New York: Citadel Press, 1971.

Burchard, Peter. *One Gallant Rush: Robert Gould Shaw and His Brave Black Regiment*. New York: Saint Martin's Press, 1965.

Cheek, William, and Aimee Lee Cheek. *John Mercer Langston and the Fight for Black Freedom, 1829–65*. Urbana: University of Illinois Press, 1989.

Clark, Peter H. *The Black Brigade of Cincinnati*. New York: Arno Press, 1969.

Cornish, Dudley Taylor. *The Sable Arm: Negro Troops in the Union Army, 1861–1865*. Edited by Herman Hattaway. Manhattan: University Press of Kansas, 1990.

Curry, Leonard P. *The Free Black in Urban America, 1800–1850: The Shadow of the Dream*. Chicago: University of Chicago Press, 1981.

Davis, John P., ed. *The American Negro Reference Book*. Englewood Cliffs, N.J.: Prentice-Hall, 1966.

Emilio, Luis F. *A Brave Black Regiment: History of the Fifty-fourth Regiment of Massachusetts Volunteer Infantry*. Boston: Boston Book Company, 1891.

Fletcher, Robert S. *A History of Oberlin College from Its Foundation through the Civil War*. Oberlin, Ohio: Oberlin College, 1943.

Franklin, John Hope. *From Slavery to Freedom: A History of American Negroes*. New York: Alfred A. Knopf, 1947.

Gladstone, William A., *Men of Color.* Gettysburg, Penn.: Thomas Publications, 1993.

———. *United States Colored Troops, 1863–1867.* Gettysburg, Penn.: Thomas Publications, 1990.

Glatthaar, Joseph T. *Forged in Battle: The Civil War Alliance of Black Soldiers and White Officers.* New York: Free Press, 1990; Meridian, 1991.

———. "Black Glory: The African-American Role in Union Victory." In *Why the Confederacy Lost,* edited by Gabor S. Boritt. New York: Oxford University Press, 1992.

Gragg, Rod. *Confederate Goliath: The Battle of Fort Fisher.* New York: HarperCollins, 1991.

Hanson, John Wesley. *Biography of William Henry Ryder, D.D.* Boston: Universalist Publishing House, 1891.

Hargrove, Hondon B. *Black Union Soldiers in the Civil War.* Jefferson, N.C.: McFarland and Company, 1988.

Hickok, Charles T. *The Negro in Ohio, 1802–1870.* 1896. Reprint, New York: AMS Press, 1975.

Higginson, Thomas W. *Army Life in a Black Regiment.* 1890. Reprint, East Lansing: Michigan State University Press, 1960.

Johnson, Jennifer, ed. *Milton M. Holland: Panola County Recipient of the Medal of Honor.* Gary, Tex.: Loblolly, 1992.

King, Susie Taylor. *Reminiscences of My Life in Camp.* 1902. Reprint, New York: Arno Press, 1968.

Langston, John M. *From the Virginia Plantation to the National Capitol.* 1894. Reprint, New York: Arno Press, 1969.

McPherson, James M. *Battle Cry of Freedom: The Civil War Era.* Cambridge: Oxford University Press, 1988; New York: Ballantine Books, 1989.

———. *The Negro's Civil War: How American Negroes Felt and Acted during the War for the Union.* New York: Pantheon Books, 1965.

Nalty, Bernard C. *Strength for the Fight: A History of Black Americans in the Military.* New York: Free Press, 1986.

Phisterer, Frederick. *Statistical Record of the Armies of the United States.* New York: Charles Scribner's Sons, 1883.

Redkey, Edwin S., ed. *A Grand Army of Black Men: Letters from African-American Soldiers in the Union Army, 1861–1865.* New York: Cambridge University Press, 1992.

Robertson, William Glenn. *Back Door to Richmond: The Bermuda Hundred Campaign, April-June 1864.* Newark: University of Delaware Press, 1987.

Snider, Wayne L. *All in the Same Spaceship: Portions of American Negro History Illustrated in Highland County, Ohio, U.S.A.* New York: Vantage Press, 1974.

Sommers, Richard J. *Richmond Redeemed: The Siege at Petersburg.* Garden City, N.J.: Doubleday, 1981.

Voegeli, V. Jacque. *Free but Not Equal: The Midwest and the Negro during the Civil War.* Chicago: University of Chicago Press, 1970.

Wesley, Charles H. *Ohio Negroes in the Civil War.* Publication no. 6, Ohio Civil War Centennial Commission. Columbus: Ohio State University Press, 1962.

Wheeler, Richard. *On Fields of Fury: From the Wilderness to the Crater, An Eyewitness History.* New York: HarperCollins, 1991.

Woodson, Carter G. *The Negro in Our History.* Washington, D.C.: Associated Publishers, 1922.

Articles

Blassingame, John W. "The Selection of Officers and Non-Commissioned Officers of Negro Troops in the Union Army, 1863–1865." *Negro History Bulletin* 30, no. 1 (1967): 8–11.

———. "The Union Army as an Educational Institution for Negroes, 1862–1865." *Journal of Negro Education* 34, no. 2 (1965): 152–59.

Carle, Glenn L. "The First Kansas Colored." *Civil War Chronicles* 3, no. 3 (1994): 54–64.

Cimprich, John, and Robert C. Mainfort Jr. "Fort Pillow Revisited: New Evidence about an Old Controversy." *Civil War History* 28, no. 4 (1982): 293–306.

Dyer, Brainerd. "The Treatment of Colored Union Troops by the Confederates, 1861–1865." *Journal of Negro History* 20, no. 3 (1935): 273–86.

Levstik, Frank. "Fifth Regiment, United States Colored Troops." *Northwest Ohio Quarterly* 30, no. 2 (1957): 20–29.

Marvin, Ulysses. "General Shurtleff." *Oberlin Alumni Magazine* 7, no. 9 (1911): 321.

Merrill, James M. "The Fort Fisher and Wilmington Campaign: Letters from Rear Admiral David P. Porter." *North Carolina Historical Review* 35, no. 4 (1958): 467–70.

Oates, Stephen B. "The Slaves Freed." *American Heritage* 32, no. 1 (1980): 74–83.

Shannon, Fred A. "The Federal Government and the Negro Soldier, 1861–1865." *Journal of Negro History* 11, no. 4, (1926): 563–83.

Sheerler, J. Reuben. "The Struggle of the Negro in Ohio for Freedom." *Journal of Negro History* 31, no. 2 (1946): 208–26.

Topping, Edgar A. "Humbly They Served: The Black Brigade in Defense of Cincinnati." *Journal of Negro History* 1 (1916): 302–17.

Wiley, Bell I. "Billy Yank and the Black Folk." *Journal of Negro History* 36, no. 1 (1951): 35–52.

Wilson, Catherine. "The 54th and 55th Regiments of Massachusetts Infantry." *Ohio Genealogical Society Report* 34, no. 3 (1994): 139–49.

Dissertations and Theses

Black, Lowell Dwight. "The Negro Volunteer Militia Units of the Ohio National Guard, 1870–1954: The Struggle for Military Recognition and Equality in the State of Ohio." Ph.D. diss., Ohio State University, 1976.

Cheek, William Francis III. "Forgotten Prophet: The Life of John Mercer Langston." Ph.D. diss., University of Virginia, 1961.

INDEX

Abolitionism, 3, 4, 5, 8, 9
Allen, Lyman, surgeon, 22–23
Andrew, John A., Gov., 9, 10
Army of the James, 52

Beatty, Powhatan, 1st Sgt., 56
Birney, William, Maj. Gen., 52, 56–57
Black Brigade of Cincinnati, 8–9
Blood, Erastus, Capt., 47–48
Board of Examination for Officers in
    USCT, 18, 19
Bragg, Braxton, Gen., 69, 71
Brazie, William R., Maj., 62, 69
Brockway, Orlando, Capt., 44
Bronson, James, 1st Sgt., 56
Butler, Benjamin F., Maj. Gen.:
    mentioned, 7; sends troops
    to confiscate rebel property,
    33; moves Army of the James
    against Petersburg, 42; reaction to
    storming of New Market Heights,
    56; assigns new officers in 5th
    USCT, 60–61; failure at Fort Fisher,
    65–68; relieved of command, 68

Camp Delaware, Ohio: Location of
    mustering, 1, 12, 16, 27; Gov.
    Tod visits, 19, 31; presentation of
    colors at, 19; training routine at,
    28; sickness at, 30
Chaplain, 21–22, 36, 64. See also
    Religion
Cleveland, Ohio, 2, 3, 6, 10
Cock, George, Capt., 34
Combat, 33, 34, 41, 42–43, 52–60,
    63, 69. See also individual battles
Conine, James, Col.: named
    commander, 19; connections in
    Kentucky, 20; leads raid into North
    Carolina, 33; use of punishment,

35; soldier as personal servant, 36;
    takes sick leave, 45
Contraband Laws, 7. See also Slaves,
    confiscation of
Cook, John B., Lt. Col., 62, 74–75
Cowles, John, Rev., 36

Daniel Webster, sinking of, 72
Davis, Jefferson, Pres.: plan to
    capture, 37
Dennison, William, Gov., 2, 30–31
Desertion, 24, 37, 47
Discipline, 35, 75
Douglass, Frederick: quoted, 16
Draper, Alonzo, Col., 53–55, 61
Duncan, Samuel, Col., 37, 42–43,
    53–54

"Ebony Tooters," 73–74
Eighteenth Corps, 40
Elections, 63–64
Emancipation Proclamation, 9

Fahrion, Gustave, Capt., 25–26
First South Carolina Volunteer
    Regiment, 8
Fort Fisher, N.C.: expeditions to,
    65–68, 69–70
Fort Gilmer, Va., 57–59, 60
Fort Pillow, reaction to, 40
Free blacks, 14–15
Freedmen, 75. See also Desertion

Grabill, Elliott, Capt., 46, 62, 70
Grant, Ulysses S., Lt. Gen., 40, 42,
    44, 50, 66, 68
Guerrillas, 33

Hinks, E. W., Gen., 44
Holland, Milton, 1st Sgt., 15, 45, 79.
    See also Medal of Honor

111